How Christians Grow

How Christians Grow

——— Spiritual Transformation for Life ———

Andrew James Prince

WIPF & STOCK · Eugene, Oregon

HOW CHRISTIANS GROW
Spiritual Transformation for Life

Copyright © 2022 Andrew James Prince. All rights reserved. Except for brief quotations in critical publications or reviews, no part of this book may be reproduced in any manner without prior written permission from the publisher. Write: Permissions, Wipf and Stock Publishers, 199 W. 8th Ave., Suite 3, Eugene, OR 97401.

Wipf & Stock
An Imprint of Wipf and Stock Publishers
199 W. 8th Ave., Suite 3
Eugene, OR 97401

www.wipfandstock.com

PAPERBACK ISBN: 978-1-6667-3844-5
HARDCOVER ISBN: 978-1-6667-9916-3
EBOOK ISBN: 978-1-6667-9917-0

09/13/22

Unless otherwise indicated all Scripture quotations are taken from The Holy Bible, New International Version® NIV®. Copyright © 1973, 1978, 1984, 2011 by Biblica, Inc.™ All rights reserved worldwide.

Scripture quotations marked "ESV" are from The Holy Bible, English Standard Version® (ESV®). Copyright © 2001 by Crossway, a publishing ministry of Good News Publishers. All rights reserved.

To my beautiful wife and fellow partner in spiritual transformation, Susan, and my greatly loved sons Nathan, Matthew, and Joshua.

Contents

Acknowledgments | ix
Prologue | xi

1. What is Spiritual Formation? | 1
2. The Means of Spiritual Formation | 11
3. Introducing the Spiritual Disciplines | 18
4. Essential Spiritual Disciplines | 24
5. Further Disciplines of the Christian Life | 35
6. Spiritual Gifts | 46
   Conclusion | 60

   Bibliography | 63

Acknowledgments

BOOKS LIKE THIS ARE never written without a context. I have been teaching on spiritual formation since joining the faculty at Brisbane School of Theology in 2009 and so thank all the students whom I have had in those classes as we have discussed, wrestled with, and prayed through this material together. This work is much richer because of you. I am particularly grateful to Talia Morris, who first suggested including Spiritual Gifts as a part of the course and led me to research this at greater depth.

I am very thankful to the Board of Brisbane School of Theology for granting me a semester of study leave in 2019 that provided me the space and time to do more extensive reading, reflecting, and writing on this topic and ultimately led to the writing of this book.

I am also grateful to Susan Chapman, John Coulson, Simon Longdon, Susan Prince, Kevin Town, and Wally Wang for reading through drafts of this book. Thankyou for being my "human laboratory" by helping me think through the material more clearly, including its practical application.

Most of all I am deeply grateful to my family, who are the crucible for this transformation into Christlikeness being experienced and lived out. Without you this work would be far less than it is.

Prologue

THE BIBLE USES MANY metaphors for the transition that occurs at the moment of Christian conversion. For example, from spiritual death to spiritual life (Eph 2:1, 5); from slaves to sin to slaves to righteousness (Rom 6:15–23); from lost to found (Luke 15:6); and from enemies of God to friends of God (Eph 2:3; Rom 5:1). But in 2 Corinthians 3, where Paul contrasts the old covenant of the Law with the glorious new covenant of Christ, he writes, "Even to this day when Moses is read, a veil covers their hearts. But whenever anyone turns to the Lord, the veil is taken away" (2 Cor 3:15–16). Like having the blindfold removed at a surprise party, at conversion the Holy Spirit removes our spiritual blindfold and we begin to see things with a spiritual clarity that we never could before (2 Cor 3:18). This raises the question though as to what happens next. Paul's explanation comes in that same verse: "And we all, with unveiled face, beholding the glory of the Lord, are being transformed into the same image from one degree of glory to another" (ESV). That is, we begin a lifetime journey of transformation into the likeness of Christ. And just in case we are tempted to think we can somehow bring about this transformation ourselves, Paul adds that this transformation comes from the Lord (2 Cor 3:18).

Have you ever considered *how* God brings about this transformation—the *means* God uses to grow Christians? How this growth begins, and how it continues? If you're a Christian reading this, can I ask you more personally: how do you continue growing spiritually when you have been a Christian for a while? How do you prevent the practice of the spiritual discipline of meditating on God's word from becoming mechanical when you have read through the Bible many times? How do you learn to pray? How do you persist in prayer when you have lived long enough to experience things that you have prayed for many times not come to pass? How do you remain sensitive to personal sin when it has been years since you've done something you are really ashamed of? How do you continue being conformed to the image of Christ for the rest of your life rather than simply putting your spiritual gearstick into neutral and coasting into eternity?

As someone who has been a Christian for many years, and who has more years behind him than ahead of him, these questions are not hypothetical, but personal. On my best days I revel in God's glorious gospel, long to spend even more time with him in fervent prayer, treat my family with kindness and compassion, and unashamedly share the gospel with unbelieving friends and acquaintances. On many days, however, I find myself untouched by the words of Scripture, distracted in prayer, thinking ill of people who I perceive have wronged me, and focused on daily circumstances rather than the return of the Lord Jesus.

If any of this resonates with you, then I encourage you to keep reading. For this is a book written by a fellow traveler who longs to finish the Christian life strongly rather than simply limp to the finish line. It is written both for newer believers as well as mature ones. It is written for those who have made enough mistakes to know they are still capable of making more and yet desire to live increasingly in holiness while still feeling the pull of the sinful nature. This book aims to give hope—both to the weary and the strong—that through the means of grace God provides they can continue growing as Christians, or resume growing if their growth has slowed or stunted.

The book first explores the *contours* of this spiritual journey of transformation into the likeness of Christ before introducing the *means* God uses to bring this about: the Holy Spirit, people, circumstances, suffering, practice of spiritual disciplines, and the use of spiritual gifts. Each of these means are then expanded upon and illustrated. The book aims to be practical with ideas and suggestions that one might apply quickly. My prayer as I have been writing is simply that in reading it you will grow more like Christ.

Chapter 1

What is Spiritual Formation?

Transformation into Christ's Image

Introduction

THE WORDS "SPIRITUAL" OR "spirituality" are used commonly in our twenty-first-century world.[1] While two thousand years of the Christian faith has traditionally confined spirituality to the realm of the professing Christian and the gathered corporate Christian community, in recent decades spirituality has become more mainstream. It has moved from the sacred to the secular. To put it another way, spirituality can now be accessed without reference to the sacred, with spiritual growth likened to personal development—"the making of a better me"—with the individual controlling this personal growth through their own activity.[2]

This is in stark contrast to the biblical view. The Bible does not use the term "spirituality" but does describe the spiritual person and what it means to live out the spiritual life. The spiritual person is one who is born of the Holy Spirit (John 3:5–8; Rom 8:2–9;

---

1. Demarest, *Satisfy Your Soul*, 7; Willard, *Renovation*, ch. 1.

2. Willard, *Renovation*, ch. 1. Marjorie Thompson develops this idea when she writes, "More and more people are separating their spirituality from religion. 'Institutional religion' has acquired strongly negative connotations, like the repellent end of a magnet. In line with our cultural individualism, people find it natural to devise private belief systems independent of historical faith communities or doctrines. Many seekers, especially among those who claim no religious affiliation, consider themselves spiritual but not religious." Thompson, *Soul Feast*, ch. 1.

1 Cor 2:15–16; 1 John 2:20; 4:2–6). The hallmark of the spiritual person is that their behavior accords with that of the Spirit himself who brings about this spiritual transformation (Rom 6:16–18; 8:5–17; Gal 5:16–26). The spiritual life, then, is having God's Spirit increasingly take control of a person's life so that they think, speak, and act like the Lord Jesus (John 3:20–21; Rom 5:1–5; 6:5–14; 8:1–11, 28–29; Gal 5:16–25; Eph 4:17–32; 5:3–5; Col 3:1–17; 1 Thess 5:23–24; 1 Tim 3:14–15; 4:7–10; 2 Tim 2:14–15, 22–26).

Spiritual Transformation

Spiritual transformation is initiated at the moment of conversion and therefore is grounded in a Christian's election and status as God's redeemed child and a coheir with Christ (Rom 8:16–17; Eph 1:3–14). As this transformation proceeds over time, spiritual growth occurs. It is concerned with lives redeemed, fueled, and surrendered to the Holy Spirit. Furthermore, "[t]he purpose of Christian spiritual formation is relationship and likeness to the person of Christ, [and] the conformity of our [lives] as [both] community and individuals to the wonderful life and message of Christ."[3] The foundation of the spiritual life for the Christian is the redeeming work of Christ himself, with justification and sanctification flowing from this union with Christ. There is no true spiritual life outside of Christ.[4] John Calvin expands on this union with Christ when he writes,

> Christ lives in us two ways. The one life consists in governing us by his Spirit, and directing all our actions; the other, in making us partakers of his righteousness, so that while we can do nothing of ourselves, we are accepted in the sight of God.[5]

---

3. Howard, *Guide*, 14.

4. "[I]t is impossible even to begin living the Christian life, or to know anything of true spirituality, before one is a Christian." Schaeffer, *True Spirituality*, 3.

5. Calvin, *Commentaries*, 74.

WHAT IS SPIRITUAL FORMATION?

The Lord by his Spirit bestows upon us the blessings of being one with him in soul and body and spirit. The bond of that connection therefore is the spirit of Christ who unites us to him and is a kind of channel by which everything that Christ has is given to us.[6]

As will be expanded upon, the process of spiritual formation is initiated and driven by the Holy Spirit, not by human action. Humanity was created in the image and likeness of God—a likeness that has been distorted since the sin of Adam and Eve (Gen 1:26; 3:1–19; 4:8–12, 23–24). Jesus is the image of the invisible God (Col 1:15). At conversion the Christian is "clothed with Christ" and has his righteousness imputed to them (2 Cor 5:21; Gal 3:26–27). In Christ our humanity is redeemed and restored so that the image of our creator begins to emerge with increasing clarity. In Christ we are reshaped according to the pattern we were created to bear (2 Cor 3:17–18).[7] This reshaping is the basic meaning of spiritual formation and refers to a Christian increasingly reflecting their status of being "in Christ" and a child of God. In spiritual formation, as we use the freedom given to us in Christ by the Spirit, we choose to submit to the Spirit's leading. In doing so we increasingly become what we were originally created to be. Having been indwelt by the Spirit at conversion, the Spirit continues that work of fashioning us into the image of Christ.

Spiritual formation (or spiritual *trans*formation as Dallas Willard prefers as a term) involves a renovation of the heart and is humanity's greatest need.[8] He notes, "[T]he only hope of humanity lies in the fact that, as our spiritual dimension has been *formed*, so it can also be *transformed*."[9] This transformation is, "a revolution of *character*, which proceeds by changing people from the inside through an ongoing personal relationship to God in Christ and to one another. It is one that changes their ideas, beliefs, feelings, and

---

6. Calvin, *Institutes* 4.17.12.
7. Schaeffer, *True Spirituality*, 4.
8. Willard, *Renovation*, 14.
9. Willard, *Renovation*, 14. Emphasis his.

habits of choice, as well as their bodily tendencies and social relations. It penetrates to the deepest layers of the soul."[10]

The New Testament speaks about spiritual growth in a number of different ways. Paul commends the Thessalonians for the abundant and continuing growth of their faith (2 Thess 1:3). To the saints in Ephesus, Paul states how God has given the church the gifts of people (apostles, prophets, evangelists, pastors, and teachers) for the purpose of equipping the saints and seeing the church built up to spiritual maturity, which he defines as attaining "unity in the faith and in the knowledge of the Son of God and become mature, attaining to the whole measure of the fullness of Christ" (Eph 4:13). He adds that this spiritual growth should be the goal for every Christian and that, as members of the body of Christ, they are to "grow to become in every respect the mature body of him who is the head, that is, Christ" (Eph 4:15). As each part of the body of Christ is functioning properly, spiritual growth of the whole body results (Eph 4:16).

In addressing factions that had arisen in the Corinthian church which demonstrated the believers' spiritual immaturity, Paul reminds the Corinthians that any growth that occurs is the result of God's work—not human effort (1 Cor 3:1–7). They are like a field—reliant on the farmer to so work the soil in order that growth results (1 Cor 3:9). And while Paul may not have seen much evidence of spiritual growth in them to that point, he has high hopes that their faith will grow in the future (2 Cor 10:15).

To the saints in Colossae, Paul adapts the metaphor of the church being like a human body with Christ as the head. Just as a body cannot grow without a head, so the church cannot grow apart from Christ. As the church avoids becoming sidetracked by irrelevant issues or ungodly behavior it remains attached to its spiritual head "from whom the whole body, supported and held together by its ligaments and sinews, grows as God causes it to grow" (Col 2:19). This further highlights the relationship between godliness

---

10. Willard, *Renovation*, 15. Emphasis his. Howard similarly states that the spiritual transformation of the believer involves not simply improving "a few habits but a renovation of our character." Howard, *Guide*, 12.

and spiritual growth and that the origin of spiritual growth is God, not ourselves. In addition, Paul urges the Colossians to actively pursue growth in their knowledge of the Lord Jesus through living in such a way that reflects the Lord's character and is fully pleasing to him (Col 1:10; 2 Pet 3:18). This leads us to consider more clearly what is meant by spiritual formation.

Defining Christian Spiritual Formation

Many definitions for spiritual formation have been offered,[11] a selection of which are included below:[12]

i. "Conformation to the image of Christ by the indwelling of the Holy Spirit."[13]

ii. "The Spirit-driven process of forming the inner world of the human self in such a way that it becomes like the inner being of Christ himself . . . Its goal is an obedience or conformity to Christ that arises out of an inner transformation accomplished through purposive interaction with the grace of God in Christ."[14]

iii. "The inner transformation of our lives."[15]

iv. "Our continuing response to the reality of God's grace shaping us into the likeness of Jesus Christ, through the work of the Holy Spirit, in the community of faith, for the sake of the world."[16]

---

11. McRay et al, "Spiritual Formation," 272, 274n11.

12. A number of these definitions are also quoted in Howard, *Guide*, 16.

13. Thompson, *Soul Feast*, ch. 1.

14. Willard, *Renovation*, 21–22. He further writes, "Spiritual formation in the tradition of Jesus Christ is the process of transformation of the inmost dimension of the human being, the heart, which is the same as the spirit or will. It is being formed (really, transformed) in such a way that its natural expression comes to be the deeds of Christ done in the power of Christ." http://www.dwillard.org/articles/individual/spiritual-formation-what-it-is-and-how-it-is-done.

15. Foster, *Celebration of Discipline*, 11.

16. Greenman, "Spiritual Formation," 24.

v. "[A] Spirit- and human-led process by which individuals and communities mature in relationship with the Christian God (Father, Son, and Holy Spirit) and are changed into ever-greater likeness to the life and gospel of this God."[17]

vi. "A process of being conformed to the image of Christ for the sake of others."[18]

An examination of these various definitions realizes a number of consistent themes and emphases regarding spiritual formation that are particularly reflected in Mulholland's definition (see above):[19]

i. It is a *process* not an *event*.

The word "process" characterizes the majority of these definitions. While specific events may contribute to a person's spiritual formation (e.g., challenge from Scripture, insights from a mentor, answered prayer, conferences), spiritual formation is a process that occurs over time. The culture of instant gratification characteristic of Western society at large has seeped its way into the church. Even Christians clamour for instant change and growth, with many books and products on the market offering various techniques designed to quickly transport us to a new realm of spiritual maturity and wholeness.

While some of these programs or techniques may be beneficial and at times result in the advancement of personal spiritual growth, there is still much about spiritual formation that is developmental. Spiritual growth, like physical growth, occurs over time. Physical growth does not always occur at a systematic rate, with periods of rapid change (e.g., infancy, puberty) interspersed with

---

17. Howard, *Guide*, 18.
18. Mulholland, *Invitation to a Journey*, 16.
19. Mulholland unpacks this definition in *Invitation to a Journey*, 23–53, under four headings: the process; being formed; image of Christ; for the sake of others. I have adapted these headings and expanded upon them.

periods of seemingly little change.[20] The same is true regarding spiritual growth. Rapid growth spurts are interspersed with often long periods of seemingly little, if any, change. Nevertheless, even during these spiritually dry or difficult periods, God is working deep down below the surface of our hearts in ways that we don't see, preparing the ground for a new season of spiritual growth.[21] As Scottish author George MacDonald aptly states:

> To give us the spiritual gift we desire, God may have to begin far back in our spirit, in regions unknown to us, and do much work that we can be aware of only in the results . . . In the gulf of our unknown being God works behind our consciousness. With His holy influence, with His own presence . . . He may be approaching our consciousness from behind, coming forward through regions of our darkness into our light, long before we begin to be aware that He is answering our request, has answered it, and is visiting His child.[22]

Spiritual formation is a journey that begins at the moment of conversion and continues throughout the whole of the Christian life. At no point does someone "arrive" at spiritual maturity and have no more to learn, grow or change. Everything we do—every thought, word, and action, along with everything that happens to us, shapes us little by little. Mulholland adds, "We are being shaped into either the wholeness of the image of Christ or a horribly destructive caricature of that image—destructive not only to ourselves but also to others, for we inflict our brokenness upon them."[23] Spiritual formation is a process that occurs over time with the end result of that process significantly influenced by our responses to the Holy Spirit as he is at work in our lives.

---

20. Mulholland, *Invitation to a Journey*, 25.

21. Mulholland, *Invitation to a Journey*, 25.

22. MacDonald, "Man's Difficulty," 329–30, quoted in Mulholland, *Invitation to a Journey*, 26.

23. Mulholland, *Invitation to a Journey*, 28.

ii. It is *being* conformed rather than *conforming ourselves*.

Nearly all of the considered definitions emphasize spiritual formation as a Spirit-driven process of *being* conformed rather than *conforming ourselves* to the image of Christ. The Spirit is the agent of formation. This point is crucial to understanding the nature of spiritual formation because what lies behind it is the issue of control.[24] We are committed to controlling every aspect of our lives and recoil from reliance or dependence on others—even God. Therefore, it is tempting to think that we can be in control of our spiritual development such as setting its direction, limits, and parameters. We can even feel comfortable with the concept of spiritual formation as long as we are in charge of it. What we struggle with is letting God take control of the process. As Mulholland concludes, "In the final analysis there is nothing we can do to transform ourselves into persons who love and serve as Jesus did except make ourselves available for God to do that work of transforming grace in our lives."[25] He later adds, "Spiritual formation is the great reversal: from acting to bring about the desired results in our lives to being acted upon by God and responding in ways that allow God to bring about God's purposes."[26] The first step in spiritual formation is being prepared to let go of the vicelike grip that we seek to maintain on our lives in general, and our spiritual development in particular. Rather than seeking to gain *from* God, the posture of spiritual formation is one of pilgrims on an uncharted journey yielding *to* God.

Howard's definition does highlight something of the human element in the spiritual formation process, but it also affirms that the Spirit is the primary agent in this process.[27] Nevertheless, Christians do have a role to play in their own spiritual growth and that of fellow believers, but it is subservient *to* and in cooperation

---

24. Mulholland, *Invitation to a Journey*, 32.
25. Mulholland, *Invitation to a Journey*, 32.
26. Mulholland, *Invitation to a Journey*, 30–31.
27. Howard, *Guide*, 17, 70–73.

with the Spirit.[28] As the believer actively submits to the will of the Spirit, lives by the Spirit, develops and maintains helpful spiritual practices, and lives in sensitive obedience to God's word—they accelerate the transforming work of God in their lives.[29]

iii. It is being conformed to the image *of Christ.*

Definitions including, "becoming like the inner being of Christ himself," "the believer's life and character transformed into that of Christ himself," and "changed into ever-greater likeness to the life and gospel of God" all highlight the goal of the spiritual formation as being conformed to the image of Christ. To the Corinthians Paul reminds them that they are being transformed into the image of God (2 Cor 3:17–18). Similarly, to the Colossians, he writes that at conversion the Christian takes off the "old self" and puts on the "new self" which is being fashioned into the image of its creator God (Col 3:9–10). Furthermore, to the Ephesians, Paul argues that God has given the church gifts of people who administer his word so that the church reaches maturity—the fullness of Christ (Eph 4:11–14).

Eph 1:3–6 makes clear that God's intention for the Christian stretches back before the foundation of the world. The believer is chosen in Christ for a purpose—so that they would be holy and blameless before their almighty heavenly Father.[30] It is at the points in our lives where we personally are most unlike the image of Christ where the deepest transformation into Christlikeness takes place.[31] As we are challenged by God's word, or by a fellow sister or brother in Christ, or are confronted by the effect of our own personal sinfulness on others, we face a choice: either we confront our sinfulness or we reject it. It is only through

---

28. Howard, *Guide*, 73–80.
29. Howard, *Guide*, 73–76.
30. Mulholland, *Invitation to a Journey*, 43.
31. Mulholland, *Invitation to a Journey*, 45.

submission to the guidance of God's Spirit, however, that spiritual transformation and renewal occur.

iv. It is both individual *and* corporate.

Spiritual formation was never meant to occur in isolation but in the context of and for the sake of the Christian community and the world. The Christian life is intensely relational, reflecting the character of the Trinitarian God. Christianity has historically tended to individualize and privatize spiritual growth (e.g., hermits living in austere conditions seeking to grow closer to God). Mulholland summarizes: "[F]or most people spiritual life and growth towards wholeness have their focus in God and self. A focus on others is rarely at the same level. Relationships with others are often seen as secondary and tangential to the primary relationship with God."[32]

If Christians are to grow holistically into the image of Christ, they must fight against this individualistic tendency. A Christian's spirituality needs to be worked out in the context of others. Every conversation, every interaction with another, becomes an opportunity for spiritual growth. Furthermore, personal ungodliness negatively impacts the body of Christ. Therefore, *personal* transformation into Christlikeness will result in a greater degree of *corporate* Christlike transformation. Such will be the effect that not only will the church be transformed but, as Greenman's definition highlights, so will society at large.

Bringing together these different elements for spiritual formation, I will offer a working definition of spiritual formation that will function as a guide for this book. Spiritual formation is *a Spirit-led and believer-response process whereby individuals and communities grow into ever-greater Christlikeness in the community of and for the sake of the church and the world.*

---

32. Mulholland, *Invitation to a Journey*, 51.

Chapter 2

The Means of Spiritual Formation

God's plan and purpose for every Christian is that they are conformed to the image of his Son (Rom 8:29). When Jesus appears in glory and the Christian receives their heavenly body, that transformation process will be complete (1 John 3:2; cf. John 3:3–8). As Christians live in the "now-but-not-yet" reality, what this means is that their lives are on a trajectory of increasing Christlikeness—of growing in godliness.[1] The triune God uses six main ways to bring about growth in godliness: the Holy Spirit, people, circumstances, suffering, practice of the spiritual disciplines and use of spiritual gifts—which will each be considered in turn.[2]

The Holy Spirit

We have previously outlined how the Spirit is an *agent* for spiritual growth, but to that we can add he is also a *means* for growth. Simply having the Spirit doesn't guarantee spiritual growth. Rather, it is our response to the Spirit's influence that significantly impacts our spiritual transformation. We can respond to the Spirit in one of two ways—either with consent or resistance.[3] We demonstrate consent when we receive the Spirit, are compelled by the Spirit,

---

1. Whitney, *Spiritual Disciplines*, 2.
2. Whitney refers to three: people, circumstances, and the spiritual disciplines. Whitney, *Spiritual Disciplines*, 10–13.
3. Howard, *Guide*, 105.

walk by the Spirit, and live according to the Spirit (Acts 20:22; Phil 3:3; Gal 5:16, 25). Conversely, we can show resistance to the Spirit's influence as we grieve, quench, lie to or test the Spirit (Acts 5:3, 9; 7:51; Eph 4:30; 1 Thess 5:19).[4] Howards adds,

> While responses of consent exhibit a kind of softness and pliability when encountering the Spirit's influence, responses of resistance exhibit a hardness, an unwillingness, or an avoidance when faced with the Spirit's active presence in the life of a community or individual. The Spirit is always an *agent* of spiritual transformation: initiating, bringing thoughts to the mind or impulses to the heart, inviting us into newness in this or that area of life. Yet it is only when we choose to pay attention and then respond to the Spirit's presence with an attitude of consent that we actually make the Spirit a means of our formation and an instrument through which we cultivate an increasing likeness to Christ and the gospel.[5]

People

People can be instrumental in our spiritual growth, both positively and negatively. Godly pastors, leaders, parents, family members, friends, mentors, congregants, and the like can be a source of knowledge, encouragement, support, advice, and models for what godliness looks like in practice. For example, it is one thing to know that one of the fruits of the Spirit is patience, but to see a parent lovingly deal with a persistently crying child, or a rebellious child week-in, week-out, demonstrates what patience looks like in the Christian life. Or when a spiritual mentor asks us how we are going in regard to a particular sin or temptation that we have shared with them leading to a time of confession and restoration, or rejoicing, or ongoing watchfulness and commitment to pursuing godliness in this area, we grow in spiritual maturity. Or if someone gives generously to support Christian ministry, or

---

4. Howard, *Guide*, 105. Biblical references are listed by Howard.
5. Howard, *Guide*, 105.

models Christ to us, or is a role model in word and deed then we can be propelled forwards in our Christian growth and maturity. Conversely, working with a colleague who frustrates us or lets us down, or being mistreated by a family member, provide opportunities for us to grow in patience, love, and forgiveness. As we do, we grow up into Christ, who is our head (Eph 4:15). When we fail to respond in such ways and our sinful nature is once again exposed, causing us to respond in repentance, restoration, and faith, we discover that God is using these difficult people to expose and rub off rough edges in our lives for the purpose of our continuing sanctification.

Circumstances

God uses both positive and negative circumstances in our lives as instruments for producing spiritual growth. For example, a particular sermon, or prayer meeting, or church camp, or Christian convention may be the catalyst for making significant life decisions, giving up sinful habits, or being liberated from an incorrect perspective. Similarly, being willing to take a risk for God and trust him to work out the details can lead to greater depth of faith. That being said, if you pause and think back over your Christian life and think about times when you feel you particularly grew as a Christian, I suspect that many of these were during periods of trial and difficulty rather than during periods when life was going well. Physical ailments, financial pressures, relational strain, job loss, wayward children, bereavement, disappointment, personal sinfulness—both our own and others, and so on, can all be harnessed by God to make us more like Christ (Rom 8:29).

Suffering

While God can use many circumstances as part of our spiritual formation, circumstances that lead to suffering seem to shape us profoundly and are worth considering in greater depth. The problem of evil, and the resultant suffering it brings—whether international, national, or personal, is still a difficult issue even for the believer with a well-constructed theodicy (Ps 4:1–2; 13:1–4; Hab 1:2–4, 12–13; Matt 27:46).[6] Suffering, particularly personal suffering, can draw us *towards* our heavenly Father as we seek solace amidst the questions, confusion, even disappointment. Alternatively, it can draw us *away* from him if we blame him in bitterness of spirit (2 Cor 12:7–11; Ruth 1:12–13, 19–21). When the storms of life come, whether or not our foundation is firmly on God will have a significant part to play in the resultant effects on our spiritual life (Matt 7:24–27).

There is a remarkable variety in the types of suffering described in Scripture, along with a variety of possible responses. In *Walking with God through Pain and Suffering*, Tim Keller categorizes different forms of suffering[7]: the suffering caused by our own failures (e.g., David, 2 Sam 12:15–18); the suffering of betrayal—which can be caused by the occasion of betrayal or attacks from others (e.g., Paul, 2 Cor 11:23–29); the suffering of loss—which is suffering caused by mortality or death and which can leave you crushed with grief (e.g., Mary and Martha, John 11:17–21); and the suffering of mystery. This refers to unexplained suffering, "the mysterious, unlooked for, and horrendous suffering that most people call 'senseless'" (e.g., the sons of Korah, Ps 44:17–19, 24; Job, Job 1:1–22; 3:1–26).[8]

One of the painful but inescapable truths is that God shapes us through suffering in ways that almost nothing else can (Rom 8:28–29). Through the agency of the Spirit, pain and suffering are able to strengthen us spiritually, as well as emotionally and mentally.[9] Sufferings prove the genuineness of our faith (Jas 1:2–3; 1 Pet 1:6–9); develop patience and perseverance (Jas 1:3; 5:7–11); cause us to focus on our eternal hope (2 Cor 5:1–6; 1 Pet 1:3–5); cause us

---

6. "Theodicy" refers to a Christian's explanation for why God allows evil.
7. Keller, *Walking with God*, 205–313.
8. Keller, *Walking with God*, 211.
9. Straw, "Native Thought," 15.

THE MEANS OF SPIRITUAL FORMATION

to rely more deeply on God (2 Cor 12:7–10); and allow us both to receive and minister God's comfort to others (2 Cor 1:3–7).

When faced with suffering, three theological truths are often challenged: that God is *wise*, that God is *loving*, and that God is *sovereign*. For reasons maybe known only to God, he allows suffering to enter or impact our lives. Like Job, we may never get to know why he has allowed it, nor is it something we would generally have chosen for ourselves to experience. God is all-wise, having never made a mistake for all eternity. But simply knowing that God has sovereignly allowed suffering to happen to us, and that he is so wise that we can't possibly doubt he knows what he is doing (as Job was confronted with in Job 38–41) often isn't enough for us as it can leave us feeling cold and somewhat bitter towards God. The third truth is crucial—that God is *loving*. While we may not always feel or experience that love tangibly, it does not stop it from being true, and being comforting. God doesn't owe the Christian a trouble-free life. Keller comments:

> What if, in the future, we came to see that Jesus could not have displayed such glory and love any other way except through his (own) suffering, and that we would not be able to experience such transcendent glory, joy, and love any other way except by going through a world of suffering? And why could it not be that our future glory will actually so swallow the evil of the past that in some unimaginable way even the memory of evil won't darken our hearts, but only make us happier?[10]

If we begin to doubt God's love in the midst of suffering, we would do well to think of the incarnation and crucifixion. Both show that God knows what it is like to be human, and so can empathize with our suffering and weaknesses (Heb 4:15; 5:7). On the cross he experienced cosmic rejection and pain that far exceeds anything we will face.[11] "God has wounds."[12] In our experiences of suffering, anger, rage, and agony, God is right there

---

10. Keller, *Walking with God*, 118.
11. Keller, *Walking with God*, 120.
12. Dickson, *If I Were God*, 69. Cf. Keller, *Walking with God*, 121.

with us holding us in the injustice—weeping with us. And "when believers in Jesus suffer, he is quite literally with us in our furnace of trouble, in some way actually feeling the flames too."[13]

Spiritual Disciplines

Another means God uses to bring about spiritual transformation is through right practice of the *spiritual disciplines*. Spiritual disciplines "are practices found in Scripture that promote spiritual growth" in the life of the Christian.[14] There is no agreed list of spiritual disciplines, but a summary of three significant authors in this area provides guidance. Richard Foster categorizes the disciplines as: *inward* (meditation, prayer, fasting, and Bible study); *outward* (simplicity, solitude, submission, and service); and *corporate* (confession, worship, guidance, and celebration).[15] Dallas Willard has two categories: disciplines of *abstinence* (fasting, solitude, silence, frugality, chastity, secrecy, and sacrifice); and disciplines of *engagement* (study, worship, celebration, service, prayer, fellowship, confession, and submission).[16] Donald Whitney categorizes the disciplines as *personal* (able to be practiced alone) and *interpersonal* (practiced in the company of others).[17] He lists the disciplines as including intake of God's word, prayer, fasting, worship, evangelism, serving, stewardship, silence and solitude, journaling, and learning.[18]

---

13. Keller, *Walking with God*, 152.
14. Whitney, *Spiritual Disciplines*, 4. Whitney, 8, adds that the purpose of practicing the disciplines is godliness or Christlikeness.
15. Foster, *Celebration of Discipline*, 13–201.
16. Willard, *Spirit of the Disciplines*, 156–92.
17. Whitney, *Spiritual Disciplines*, 5.
18. Whitney, *Spiritual Disciplines*, 7.

Spiritual Gifts

Spiritual gifts are supernatural, God-given abilities distributed by God the Father, God the Son, and God the Holy Spirit to the Christian for the purpose of building up the body of Christ, and for unifying and edifying the church (Eph 4:12–16). God gives different gifts to different people, and all gifts are God's grace to the believer. As we lovingly use our gifts to the glory of God and for the building up of his church, so we personally grow in spiritual maturity (Rom 12:6; 1 Cor 12:11; Eph 4:11–13).

While people, circumstances, and suffering work from the outside in, the Spirit through the spiritual disciplines and spiritual gifts works from the inside out.[19] While the Christian may have limited control regarding the people or circumstances that come into their lives, they do have control over how they *respond* to these people or circumstances. Simply experiencing bereavement, unemployment, or relational conflict, for example, does not guarantee spiritual growth. Spiritual maturity develops as the Christian draws on the power and strength of the Spirit and responds in faith and godliness. Spiritual immaturity and regression occur when the believer, faced with these same circumstances, either responds to them in their own strength or responds with their flesh nature rather than their spirit nature (Gal 5:16–17). This helps explain why two believers, when faced with the same set of circumstances, may have vastly different outcomes in regard to spiritual growth. Both of them hear God's word but only one may do what it says (Matt 7:24–27; Jas 1:22).

Furthermore, while the believer may have less choice regarding the people and circumstances that come into their lives, they have a far greater degree of choice regarding practicing (or not practicing) the spiritual disciplines and using their spiritual gift(s).[20] Judicial practice of the disciplines, in particular, can provide fertile soil in which spiritual growth may occur, and so will form the subject of the next three chapters, followed by a consideration of spiritual gifts.

19. Whitney, *Spiritual Disciplines*, 10–11.
20. Whitney, *Spiritual Disciplines*, 10–11.

Chapter 3

Introducing the Spiritual Disciplines

The Nature and Purpose of the Spiritual Disciplines

WHILE THE CHRISTIAN'S TRANSFORMATION into Christlikeness will be complete at the return of Christ, the consistent refrain of Scripture is that they are not to wait for God's holiness to descend upon them. Rather, they are to actively pursue godliness (1 Thess 4:1–8; 2 Thess 2:15–17; 1 Tim 4:6–10; 2 Tim 2:1–6, 15; 3:10–15; Heb 12:14; 1 Pet 1:22–23; 4:7–10; 1 John 2:15–17; 4:7). While this can only be achieved through the agency of the Spirit, Christians are nevertheless to actively train/discipline themselves to be godly—which is where the spiritual disciplines fit in. The purpose of the spiritual disciplines is godliness in the life of the Christian, with the road to spiritual maturity and godliness coming through right practice of them.[1]

Spiritual disciplines "are *activities*, not *attitudes*."[2] Fasting is a discipline because it is a human activity (unlike things like peace, or love, or humility—which are attitudes).[3] It is also important to note that the disciplines are a means to an end, not an

---

1. Whitney, *Spiritual Disciplines*, 4, 10. Whitney, ix, explains that the word "discipline" is derived from the Latin *disciplinae*, meaning courses/practices of learning and training.
2. Whitney, *Spiritual Disciplines*, 6. Emphasis his.
3. Whitney, *Spiritual Disciplines*, 6.

end in themselves.[4] Being transformed into the image of Christ for the sake of the church and the world is the goal. Mere performance of the disciplines does not guarantee growth in godliness because the state of our hearts—including our motivations and desires—may not be Christlike. But true godliness will not ultimately be achieved apart from the disciplines, for godliness comes through discipline (1 Tim 4:7).[5] Whitney helpfully summarizes when he writes that the spiritual disciplines "are those personal and interpersonal activities given by God in the Bible as the sufficient means believers in Christ Jesus are to use in the Spirit-filled, gospel-driven pursuit of godliness, that is, closeness to Christ and conformity to Christ."[6] He further elaborates:

> Think of the Spiritual Disciplines as ways by which we can spiritually place ourselves in the path of God's grace and seek Him, much like Zacchaeus placed himself physically in Jesus' path and sought Him. The Lord, by His Spirit, still travels down certain paths, paths that He himself has ordained and revealed in Scripture. We call these paths the Spiritual Disciplines, and if we place ourselves on these paths and look for Him there by faith, we can expect to encounter Him. For instance, when we come to the Bible, or when we engage in any of the biblical Disciplines—looking by faith to God through them—we can anticipate experiencing God. As with this tax collector [Zacchaeus], we will find Him willing to have mercy on us and to have communion with us. And in the course of time we, too, will be transformed by Him from one level of Christlikeness to another (see 2 Corinthians 3:18). So again, by means of these Bible-based practices we consciously place ourselves before God in anticipation of enjoying His presence and receiving His transforming grace.[7]

---

4. Whitney, *Spiritual Disciplines*, 9.

5. Whitney, *Spiritual Disciplines*, 9–10.

6. Whitney, *Spiritual Disciplines*, 9. Following Whitney, 6, the discussion on spiritual disciplines in this book will be limited to those practices found in Scripture.

7. Whitney, *Spiritual Disciplines*, 13.

A History of the Spiritual Disciplines

Western society has imbibed the view that we have a right to the "good life"—a life of satisfaction, convenience, and prosperity. Not only that, but if we do not pursue the good life then many people would consider that there is something wrong with us.[8] The Reformation teaching of "Christ alone, Grace alone, Faith alone, and Scripture alone" has seemingly freed the Christian for the past five hundred years or so to largely ignore or disparage the practice of various spiritual disciplines. These disciplines (or practices), however, have been the very ones which have aided the spiritual formation of countless saints for at least the past three thousand years.

While practice of the disciplines has been a feature of Catholicism for two millennia, they have not been as widely embraced by Protestantism as a whole. This has been particularly due to the abuse of such practices by some Christian ascetics throughout history—most notably in the monastic movement.[9] For the first three hundred years of Christian history Christianity was a persecuted religion, which had the effect of keeping it distinct and separate from the surrounding society (to a greater or lesser degree). Following the conversion of the Roman emperor, Constantine, along with the proclamation of the Edict of Toleration and the Edict of Milan during the fourth century, Christianity began to experience security, legal standing, and imperial patronage.[10] The impact of this new status on the church was that it became less and less distinct from its society. In other words, the church became increasingly secularized.

Some who longed for a purified form of Christianity began taking to the Egyptian desert and ushered in what has become known as the monastic movement. Initially this consisted of people living by themselves in the wilderness—exposed to the elements and predators (both human and animal).[11] Many per-

---

8. Willard, *Spirit of the Disciplines*, 130–32.
9. Willard, *Spirit of the Disciplines*, 139.
10. Willard, *Spirit of the Disciplines*, 140.
11. Willard, *Spirit of the Disciplines*, 141.

INTRODUCING THE SPIRITUAL DISCIPLINES

ished in these conditions. For self-protection, some began to form themselves into monastic communities. Within the protected confines of a monastery each person had their own cell (room) which allowed them to remain living as a hermit, with minimal contact with fellow hermits, while experiencing a level of physical protection. Each of these hermits, therefore, "could safely pursue his union with God without the threats and dangers of complete desert solitude."[12]

Some of the "desert fathers" and subsequent monastics engaged in many austere practices such as: eating only uncooked food; sleeping standing up for years; allowing beetles/maggots to infest personal wounds; carrying weights anywhere a person went; living in iron chains and so on. As Dallas Willard delightfully summarizes, "[these men vied] with one another for the championship in austerities."[13]

One notable example is that of John Chrysostom. "John of Antioch, later known as *Chrysostomos* i.e. Golden Mouth, was born in or around 349, in Antioch of Syria, into a well-to-do family."[14] In his early years, prior to becoming a presbyter in Antioch (and later—bishop of Constantinople), he spent six years in the Antiochene mountains where he adopted a strict ascetic lifestyle. Historians maintain that for two of these years he had little sleep and minimal food while he committed himself to memorizing the entire Old Testament and New Testament.[15] The strictness of his regime resulted in a deterioration of his health, causing him to leave his mountain dwelling and return to a city residence in Antioch in 378.[16] For the remainder of his life, as much as he was able, Chrysostom continued to practice the "monastic austerities" he had employed in the mountains, and at heart never ceased thinking of himself as a monk.[17]

12. Willard, *Spirit of the Disciplines*, 141.
13. Willard, *Spirit of the Disciplines*, 142.
14. Prince, *Contextualization*, 135.
15. Mayer and Allen, *John Chrysostom*, 6; Kelly, *Golden Mouth*, 32.
16. Kelly, *Golden Mouth*, 32–34.
17. Kelly, *Golden Mouth*, 35.

Flagellation (both corporal and self) became an increasing monastic phenomenon, particularly from the twelfth century.[18] The ascetic practices regularly ended in abuse and spiritual degradation rather than formation of the person engaged in the ascetic activities. Ironically, such outcomes demonstrated that these ascetics were still *in* the world and *of* the world—the very things they were seeking to avoid.

With the Reformation and the advent of Protestantism, monasticism, asceticism, and the associated spiritual disciplines were largely dispensed with by Protestant Christians. Richard Lovelace summarizes by saying:

> The reformers shied away from spiritual exercises as a road to growth, though they did stress the need to hear and read Scripture in order to nourish faith and the need to pray in order to express faith. John Calvin also balanced Luther's emphasis on justification by an extensive treatment of sanctification. Out of the material in the application sections of Paul's letters, Calvin carefully drew an understanding of spiritual growth through mortification of sin and vivification of every aspect of the personality by the Spirit's releasing work. Calvin's later disciple, John Owen, went so far as to say that "the vigour and power of spiritual life are dependent on mortification of sin." The Reformed tradition thus made a strong effort to rule out cheap grace.[19]

Puritan spirituality attempted to "graft patristic and medieval spirituality onto the Reformation base of justification by grace."[20] A number of aspects of Puritan spirituality have been retained by contemporary evangelicalism including the daily "quiet time," prayer before meals, family devotions, and spiritual journals.[21]

An emphasis *on* and practice *of* the spiritual disciplines has not been a feature of Protestant Christianity since the time of

---

18. Willard, *Spirit of the Disciplines*, 143.
19. Lovelace, "Evangelical Spirituality," 29.
20. Lovelace, "Evangelical Spirituality," 30.
21. Lovelace, "Evangelical Spirituality," 30.

the Reformers. This raises the question, however, of whether the baby been thrown out with the bathwater. Has all this Protestant negativity towards asceticism caused it to inadvertently dispense with practices within the realm of spiritual disciplines that may indeed be helpful?[22] I think this may well be the case for at least some Christians. In 2 Pet 1:5–7 the apostle Peter, through the Holy Spirit, writes of making progress in the Christian life in all sorts of areas: virtue, knowledge, self-control, steadfastness, godliness, brotherly affection, and love. He proceeds to highlight *why* we should make progress in these things—namely that they stop us from becoming ineffective and unfruitful as Christians (2 Pet 1:8). Furthermore, if we don't pursue these qualities then we demonstrate our immaturity as Christians (what Peter describes as being "nearsighted and blind"), having forgotten that we have put to death our former way of life (2 Pet 1:9). This progress, or maturity in the Christian life, doesn't just happen. Rather, the Christian has an active role to play. Peter says we are to "make every effort" and to be "all the more diligent" in pursuing these qualities, for if we practice such qualities, we will be living in a way that pleases and honours our heavenly Father and will result in him richly welcoming us on the final day (2 Pet 1:5, 10, 11). The idea here is that we are to be active, diligent, thoughtful, consistent, and conscientious in our endeavours of actively pursuing righteousness.[23]

It is at this point that the spiritual disciplines come into play. A *measured* consideration of the main spiritual disciplines that have been practiced down through the centuries is in order so as to discover their usefulness (or otherwise) for the spiritual formation of the Christian today. Irrespective of what your practice is of the various spiritual disciplines referred to in this chapter, there are two disciplines which are essential for spiritual growth—meditating on (and subsequently obeying) Scripture and responding to what God has revealed through prayer. It is to these we first turn.

---

22. Cf. Miles, "New Asceticism," 1097.
23. Green, *Jude and 2 Peter*, 200.

Chapter 4

Essential Disciplines of the Christian Life

Meditative Reading of Scripture

THE OPENING CHAPTER OF the Bible presents the creator God as one who communicates with his creation through speaking (Gen 1:3, 6, 9, 11, 14, 20, 24, 26). He speaks the universe into existence and speaks to the creatures he has made (Gen 1:28–30; 3:9–19). God spoke in many different ways throughout the Old Testament period—most notably through his prophets, but ultimately revealed himself through his Word—Jesus Christ (John 1:1; Heb 1:1–2). God has left his revealed word in the Old and New Testament Scriptures through which he continues speaking to humanity today. Through the powerful work of the Holy Spirit, God's word corrects, rebukes, equips, and trains the believer for a life of righteousness and for engaging in every good work ordained by the Father (2 Tim 3:16–17). As the believer hears God's word and does what it says they remain in Christ and grow spiritually (John 15:1–5).

When we read the Bible there are two levels of understanding required. The first concerns knowledge acquired by study (e.g., context, historical setting, interpretative issues).[1] The second, however, is a deeper level, where insight is gained on a personal level. It is only when this second level is achieved that the Bible really is

---

1. For further see Chin, *How to Read*.

grasped. We are not to despise the first level, nor neglect the second. We are to reflectively assimilate God's word. As we read or hear God's word, God speaks to us. Our problem is that we are not always ready to hear what God is saying. For example, we can read the words quickly, or mentally gloss over a familiar text, or be distracted or impacted by life circumstances. The net result can be that we fail to discern all that God is revealing to us. Meditative reading of Scripture is about slowing down our intake of God's word so that we don't simply *read* it but actually meditate on it, ruminate on it, savor it, and then respond to what God has said through prayer. This doesn't negate the value or importance of reading (or hearing) larger sections of God's word. For example, if we only read and meditated on one verse of the Bible a day it would take us a long time to read through the Bible—just over eighty-five years, in fact! In doing so we would probably miss a lot of key themes and interconnections between chapters, books, and the Bible as a whole that are more readily discovered by consistently reading through whole chapters, or books at one time. Furthermore, such a slow reading would bring a greater challenge of reading and interpreting each verse in its context in relation to the verses around it, the chapter, and the book as a whole.[2] With reading the Bible we need both breadth and depth. If you read three chapters of the Bible a day you would get through it in just over a year. But having read those three chapters, you could then focus on one section out of those chapters to meditate on in particular. Breadth *and* depth in Bible reading are a staple for Christian growth and maturity.

The Scriptures themselves have much to say about the value and practice of reading the biblical text. The Bible can be said to revive the soul, give wisdom and understanding to those who seek it, bring joy to the heart, bring warning to the discerning reader, and be a lamp and guide for life (Ps 119:7–11, 105). As the breath of God, all parts of Scripture are useful for equipping the Christian for a life of service (2 Tim 3:16–17).

---

2. Chin helpfully elaborates on this issue of how to read the Bible in context. Chin, *How to Read*, 47–55.

Christian writers, both ancient and modern, have also reflected on the Christian's reading of Scripture. John Calvin is one such example, who writes,

> God has provided the assistance of the Word for the sake of all those to whom He has been pleased to give useful instruction because He foresaw that His likeness imprinted upon the most beautiful form of the universe would be insufficiently effective. Hence we must strive onward toward this straight path if we seriously aspire to the pure contemplation of God. We must come, I say, to the Word, where God is truly and vividly described to us.[3]

More recently, Robert Mulholland has likened Scripture to a lake whose depths have never been fully plumbed.[4] Like a fisherman in a small boat casting a line in the midst of a vast lake, so is the Christian when reading Scripture. We can never master Scripture, or think we have learned all there is to learn about a verse, or chapter, or book. As we contemplate or meditate on Scripture with a heart sensitized to the refining work of the Spirit, then there are always fresh things that we can learn from it.

The practice of spiritual reading is more like savoring a letter from a dear friend than scanning a newspaper. What makes reading "spiritual" is the intention, attitude, and manner in which we approach God's words. Marjorie Thomson helpfully expresses it when she says,

> Spiritual reading is reflective and prayerful. It is not concerned with speed or volume but with depth and receptivity. This is because the purpose of spiritual reading is to open ourselves to how God may be speaking to us in and through any particular text. The manner of spiritual reading is like drinking in the words of a love letter or pondering the meaning of a poem. It is not like skittering over the surface of a popular magazine or ploughing through a computer manual. We are seeking formation, not merely information. Information is

3. Calvin, *Institutes*, 1.6.3.
4. Quoted in Thompson, *Soul Feast*, ch. 2.

basically utilitarian; it is a means to some other end . . . Formation, on the contrary, is generally understood as an end in itself. It has to do with the dynamics of change in the human heart, change that reshapes us into the kind of beings God intends for us to be . . . The term *formation*, then, suggests being shaped ever more deeply according to the mind of Christ, who reveals and offers to us our full humanity. Spiritual reading has a formative intent. Through it we seek a living, transforming relationship with God-in-Christ. Spiritual reading is a meditative approach to the written word. It requires unhurried time and an open heart.[5]

When we are engaged in spiritual reading it is not so much about us reading God's word but God's word reading us (Heb 4:12–13).[6] Historically, this way of reading Scripture has more often been known by its Latin name *Lectio Divina* (which simply means "spiritual reading"). While its origins lay with St. Benedict[7] in the sixth century, even the great reformer John Calvin and the puritan pastor Richard Baxter, to name but a few, advocated a style of reading the Bible that was largely drawn from this Benedictine tradition.[8]

Lectio Divina, as it has been classically understood and practiced for centuries, has three main stages that are particularly pertinent to the Bible reader committed to a careful and context-sensitive approach to the biblical text:[9]

i. *Reading*. It is reading in a "reflective, gentle paced, one-bite-at-a-time" manner.[10] It is the sort of reading you engage in when savoring a letter from your beloved. You allow the words which

5. Thompson, *Soul Feast*, ch. 2.
6. Thompson, *Soul Feast*, ch. 2.
7. St. Benedict (480–543 AD) is considered the father of Western monasticism. As well as founding twelve communities for monks in Italy he most famously developed the "Benedictine Rule" which is a book about how monks were to live their lives and how to run a monastery efficiently.
8. Thompson, *Soul Feast*, ch. 2.
9. I am particularly drawing from Thompson, *Soul Feast*, ch. 2, for this summary of *Lectio Divina*.
10. Thompson, *Soul Feast*, ch. 2.

are significant and weighty to sink in and expand and nourish your heart, even if those words at times are painful words. As Thompson explains, "The question behind our reading [should be], God, what are you saying to me just now?"[11]

ii. *Meditation.* This is not the sort of meditation advocated by New Age thinkers or Eastern religions where you empty your mind. Rather, biblical meditation involves having an active mind. As you are reading the text (often out loud, as in a quiet murmur) you turn over the words and phrases in your mind, seeking to find connection between your own story and the great story of God's redemptive work. Meditation engages our hopes, thoughts, feelings, and desires. It is at this point where we are likely to discover what a particular passage we have been reading means for our lives personally or for the society in which we live.

iii. *Spoken prayer.* This refers to "prayer that naturally flows out of our meditation" and is our "first response to God to what we have heard and assimilated" in *reading* and *meditation*.[12] It may be prayers of adoration, thanksgiving, repentance, or petition.

The psalmist writes, "I meditate on your precepts and consider your ways. I delight in your decrees; I will not neglect your word" (Ps 119:15–16). In the end, "it is the *attitude* we bring to spiritual reading that allows God to transform the text" from simply being interesting words to being words with the power to change our hearts."[13] What is required is an attitude that expects to encounter God through his word, that is willing to listen to what he says, and that desires to respond completely to what the Spirit reveals.[14]

---

11. Thompson, *Soul Feast*, ch. 2.

12. Thompson, *Soul Feast*, ch. 2.

13. Thompson, *Soul Feast*, ch. 2.

14. Thompson, *Soul Feast*, ch. 2. Whitney, *Spiritual Disciplines*, 56–78, provides many practical suggestions for how to meditatively read and study God's word.

ESSENTIAL DISCIPLINES OF THE CHRISTIAN LIFE

To further expand on the basic *Lectio* principles of reading, meditating, and responsive prayer, Richard Chin provides some practical tips on Bible reading that can helpfully be applied to our meditative reading of Scripture, including: making careful observations from the text; asking questions of the text and then looking for answers to these from within the text; noting the genre, repeated words or phrases; identifying the context; noting any surprises in the text; and reflecting on how a particular passage points to Jesus.[15]

As I write I am currently reading through Isaiah and have been meditating on two verses from chapter 40—verses one and two: "Comfort, comfort my people, says your God. Speak tenderly to Jerusalem, and proclaim to her that her hard service has been completed, that her sin has been paid for, that she has received from the Lord's hand double for all her sins."

The context of these verses is that they are an announcement of comfort for the returnees from Babylon. There are a number of things that stood out to me as I read them. First, they are a complete contrast to the thirty-nine chapters that preceded them, which have been largely about Judah's sinfulness, warnings of pending destruction of Jerusalem, and exile of its inhabitants. Second, the phrase "my people" (v. 1) shows such graciousness from the Lord. The nation has been sinful over many years, but God hasn't disowned them. The people have fallen but God has welcomed them back into his arms (v. 11) as his people (v. 1). Third, the phrase "her sin has been paid for" speaks to how God hasn't turned a blind eye to her sin. God has punished her through seventy years in exile but now welcomes her back as a forgiven people. A fourth thing, however, that caught my attention was the phrase "double for all her sins" (v. 2). I wondered exactly what this meant as, on face value, it could seem to infer an unfairness on the part of God—that the punishment had been excessive. I couldn't work it out myself so had a quick look at a commentary which suggested simply that the verse wasn't conveying the idea of excessive punishment but rather that both Judah's obvious sins

---

15. Chin, *How to Read*, 31–38.

as well as her less obvious/hidden sins have been dealt with, and that her spiritual debt has been paid.[16]

One of the implications I drew from these two verses is that God is a holy God who doesn't ignore sin. Sin must be punished. I know that my sins are so great (and I add to them most days) and deserve much punishment from God. And yet, he has chosen me, accepted Jesus's death as punishment for all of my sins, completely forgiven me, exchanged my filthy rags for the righteous cloak of Christ, and welcomed me into his arms. Oh, what a wonderful God. Oh, what a glorious Saviour. How can I ever thank him enough? And praise him enough? This then led me to pray and record in my journal: "Oh heavenly Father. I hate every single sinful thing I have ever done. I am grieved to the core. I confess everything to you now and declare to you that I am a sinner who desperately needs a Saviour. Father, please cleanse me from all of my sins right now. I claim the cleansing blood of Jesus, which I don't deserve, and accept his forgiveness by faith. Please strengthen me by your Spirit not to sin, and to resist the temptation to sin, so that I might increasingly be transformed into your likeness. Amen."

Having my prayers informed by and flowing from my meditation on Scripture has had a significant impact on my prayer life. First, it has more naturally linked my Scripture reading and prayers rather than them being more separate activities. Second, it has helped my prayers to be more biblically informed rather than simply whatever has come out of my head. And third, it has led me to pray all sorts of things for myself and others that I would never have thought to pray except for the fact that I had read a particular passage that day. I don't know if you have this same problem, but what do you pray for someone whom you pray for regularly? In the next section I will develop this idea, but I have certain people and things that I pray for daily, others weekly, and others on a bigger list where I systematically pray through a couple of names each day. So, as I pray for my wife, each of my children and each of my pastors and their families each day, for example, what can I pray for them that is different to what I

---

16. Motyer, *Isaiah*, 243–44.

prayed for them yesterday? Or the day before? Or the week before? My default is that they will grow more like Christ and know God's strengthening in their lives and ministry—which is a reasonable default in some ways. But having my prayers informed by my Scripture reading that day has reaped enormous dividends in growing my prayer life. We will continue to explore the spiritual discipline of prayer in our next section.

Prayer

Many Christians feel guilty regarding the state of their prayer life—even long-time believers. While they may have made spiritual progress in other areas this is one essential discipline where they feel deficient—even embarrassed about. They long to grow in prayer, to look forward to times of prayer, and to enjoy praying. The good news is that this is possible. I don't think you need me to tell you to pray. Or to pray more. The purpose of this section is not to incur guilt but rather share a number of important theological statements regarding the nature of prayer mixed with some practical suggestions that might help you grow in this area of your spiritual life.

There are many fine books on prayer, which develop a theology of and practical ideas for prayer and won't look to reproduce their thoughts here.[17] Rather, I will draw on the work of just two writers who collectively provide a summary of some important theological concepts in relation to prayer, before moving onto some further practical implementation.

Tim Chester delightfully defines prayer as being like a child asking their father for help.[18] He argues that there are three key theological truths about God and prayer we need to know: "1. God the Father loves to hear us pray; 2. God the Son makes every prayer pleasing to God; 3. God the Holy Spirit helps us as we pray."[19] Cer-

---

17. For example, see: Carson, *Spiritual Reformation*; Jensen and Payne, *Prayer*; Graeme Goldsworthy, *Knowledge of God*.
18. Chester, *You Can Pray*, 16.
19. Chester, *You Can Pray*, 10.

tainly we pray to our heavenly Father to adore him, thank him, confess our sins, and pour out our troubles but prayer, at its heart, is about asking (cf. Jas 4:2). Donald Whitney's chapter on prayer as a spiritual discipline, in *Spiritual Disciplines for the Christian Life*, highlights three further principles:[20]

i. *Prayer is expected.* Jesus frequently spoke of his expectation that Christians pray (Matt 6:5, 6, 7, 9; Luke 11:9; 18:1). Likewise, Paul commands Christians to devote themselves to prayer, meaning that prayer should be a priority that they sacrifice things for (Col 4:2). Furthermore, they are to "pray continually"—meaning that they are to pray regularly throughout the day (1 Thess 5:17). Martin Luther expressed it well when he said, "As it is the business of tailors to make clothes and of cobblers to mend shoes, so it is the business of Christians to pray."[21] There are a number of reasons why Christians don't pray more than they do. Sometimes it is because they don't discipline themselves to find a regular time and place. Sometimes it's because they don't know what to say. Sometimes it's because they don't believe their prayers will make any real difference. Sometimes it's because of sin in their life, leaving them feeling too ashamed to pray. Sometimes it's just a lack of sense of the need to pray.

ii. *Prayer is learned.* Just like riding a bike or making a soufflé, prayer is something that is learned rather than being something that is necessarily inherent. Even mature Christians can grow in the practice of prayer. Our starting point is to say, in the words of Luke 11:1, "Lord, teach us to pray."[22]

iii. *Prayer is answered.* The oft-forgotten truth is that God hears and answers the prayers of his children. Sometimes we do not get the answers we want because we pray out of line with Scripture, or with selfish motives, or regarding things that

---

20. Whitney, *Spiritual Disciplines*, 79–99. For further see Chester, *You Can Pray*.

21. Quoted in Whitney, *Spiritual Disciplines*, 82.

22. Whitney, *Spiritual Disciplines*, 85.

would not glorify him. But more often we don't get answers to prayer because we simply don't ask (Jas 4:1–4).[23]

A biblically informed theology of prayer that knows our heavenly Father has made prayer possible through the atoning death and resurrection of his Son (Heb 10:19–21), that he longs to hear us pray (1 Pet 3:12), that he has given us the Holy Spirit to help us pray (Rom 8:26–27), and that he is both willing and able to answer our prayers (Mark 9:22–23), will do more to encourage us to pray and grow us in prayer than any amount of "how to" tips. But wherever you are at in your journey with prayer, as a spiritual practice it is something you can make progress in if you wish to practice being godly (1 Tim 4:8).

We have earlier reflected on the value of letting prayer naturally flow in response to what we have read in Scripture. Another way that Scripture and prayer can be linked is through praying prayers found in Scripture. Each of these prayers has a context, of course, and so it is important to be conscious of this, but learning to pray by appropriating prayers of Jesus (e.g., Matt 6:9–13; John 17:16–25), or other believers (e.g., Phil 1:9–11; Eph 3:14–21; Col 1:3–14; 1 Thess 3:9–13) can help broaden our prayers and make them more biblically informed.[24] Relatedly, various believers throughout the centuries have also recorded their prayers. Praying through the printed prayers of others (e.g., church fathers, Puritans, liturgical prayer books)[25] and praying with others who are good models in prayer can further grow us in prayer.

Conclusion

As we read and meditate on God's word, respond in prayer, and put it into practice, all through the power of the Spirit, something

---

23. Whitney, *Spiritual Disciplines*, 94–96.

24. For example, Carson, *Spiritual Reformation*, examines each of the prayers of Paul recorded in his letters and how they can be appropriated by the believer.

25. For example, Bennett, *Valley of Vision*.

remarkable begins to happen. We increasingly become like the strong, growing, vibrant, and fruitful tree described in Psalm 1. We grow more like Christ. But as we considered earlier, as part of actively training ourselves in godliness, there are other spiritual disciplines or practices that believers down through the centuries have practiced as an aid to spiritual maturity. We will consider a selection of these in our next chapter.

Chapter 5

Further Disciplines of the Christian Life

Fasting

CHRISTIAN FASTING HAS BEEN described as "the voluntary abstinence from food (some would add drink) for spiritual purposes."[1] Some people feel the freedom to use the term fasting more broadly to include abstaining or denying oneself the enjoyment of something for spiritual purposes, for example, television, screen time, sex, a hobby, sleep etc.[2] The Bible describes fasting in relation to food (and drink), and has been historically practiced this way, so we will restrict our discussion to this narrower definition.

Fasting is a discipline that was practiced by believers in both Old and New Testaments. Whitney identifies ten biblical purposes for fasting: to strengthen prayer (Ezra 8:23; Neh 1:4; Acts 13:3); to seek God's guidance (Judg 20:26–28; Acts 14:23); to express grief (1 Sam 20:34; 33:13; 2 Sam 1:11–12); to seek deliverance and

---

1. Whitney, *Spiritual Disciplines*, 192.

2. Whitney, *Spiritual Disciplines*, 193, quotes Martin Lloyd Jones: "To make the matter complete, we would add that fasting, if we conceive of it truly, must not only be confined to the question of food or drink; fasting should really be made to include abstinence from anything that is legitimate in and of itself for the sake of some special spiritual purpose. There are many bodily functions which are right and normal and perfectly legitimate, but which for special peculiar reasons in certain circumstances should be controlled. That is fasting. There, I suggest, is a kind of general definition of what is meant by fasting."

protection (Ezra 8:21–23; Ps 109:24); to express repentance and return to God (1 Sam 7:6; Joel 2:12; Jonah 3:5–8); to humble oneself before God (1 Kgs 21:27–29); to express concern for the work of God (Dan 9:3); to minister to the needs of others; to overcome temptation and dedicate oneself to God (Matt 4:1–11); and, to express love and worship to God (Luke 2:37).[3]

In the New Testament there appears to be something of an ambivalence towards fasting in the teaching of Jesus. He seems to expect that his Jewish audience would fast, yet he and his disciples do not appear to have practiced fasting either at all, or at least regularly in the manner of the disciples of John the Baptist or those of the Pharisees (Matt 6:16; 9:14; Luke 5:33). Much of the discussion regarding Christian fasting is centered on the question as to whether fasting is a direct command of Jesus or not, with the two key texts being Matt 6:16–18 and Matt 9:14–17.

Fasting appears to have been a common activity in the post-apostolic period, although it was not emphasized as a regular practice but rather saved for particular occasions (e.g., Acts 13:2; 14:23).[4] It was practiced by Christians throughout the Middle Ages but developed something of a negative reputation through ascetic abuses of it where it was often accompanied with extreme practices such as self-flagellation, sleep deprivation and self-isolation. The sixteenth-century Reformers mostly ignored the obligatory fasts of the Catholic Church. Luther was largely ambivalent about fasting and left it to an individual's conscience, while Calvin saw some positive value in fasting—although was opposed to extreme fasting (e.g., forty days) or fasting for the purpose of gaining merit before God. Fasting was common amongst the Puritans but has been by and large neglected as a regular practice by most parts of the Protestant church over the last one hundred and fifty years. There is no consensus regarding its place in the Christian church in the twenty-first century.[5] For

---

3. Whitney, *Spiritual Disciplines*, 200–217. The biblical references are from Whitney. See also Foster, *Celebration of Discipline*, 66–69.

4. Linder, "Fast, Fasting," 438.

5. Matthews summarizes the evangelical scholarly landscape on fasting by

some Christians, fasting is a regular practice. For others, the idea of fasting has rarely even been contemplated.

Silence and Solitude

Silence is "the voluntary and temporary abstention from speaking so that certain spiritual goals might be sought."[6] Solitude is the discipline of withdrawing from others *for a period of time* in order to be alone with and give undivided attention to God.[7] Solitude may be for as little as a few minutes, or for a few days.[8] Kenneth Boa argues that "solitude is the most fundamental of the disciplines in that it moves us away, for a time, from the lures and aspirations of the world into the presence of the Father. In solitude . . . we discover a place of strength, dependence, reflection, and renewal, and we confront inner patterns and forces that are alien to the life of Christ within us."[9]

While silence and solitude are distinct practices, Boa explains that "silence is the catalyst of solitude; it prepares the way for inner seclusion and enables us to listen to the quiet voice of the Spirit."[10] Similarly, Whitney argues that solitude is often (but not always) accompanied by silence.[11] A person may engage in

---

saying that there is little scholarly literature on the subject and that the practice of it amongst lay evangelicals has been mostly shaped by popular authors and speakers such as Richard Foster, Dallas Willard, Donald Whitney, Bill Bright, and Elmer Towns. Matthews credits these men and a number of others as leading something of a resurgence in the practice of fasting amongst evangelicals over the past forty years, although he largely seems to be speaking for the American evangelical scene rather than more broadly amongst Protestant evangelicalism. Matthews, *Christian Fasting*, 107, 116–17.

6. Whitney, *Spiritual Disciplines*, 224.
7. Barton, "Solitude," 762; cf. Whitney, *Spiritual Disciplines*, 225.
8. Whitney, *Spiritual Disciplines*, 225.
9. Boa, *Conformed to His Image*, 83.
10. Boa, *Conformed to His Image*, 83.
11. Whitney, *Spiritual Disciplines*, 225. Richard Foster argues that solitude must be accompanied by silence in order for it to be true solitude. Foster, *Celebration of Discipline*, 122.

solitude while still reading or praying out loud or with music or other noise in the background. Silence, however, is "withdrawing or abstaining from noise, words, and activity for a time to become more attuned to the voice of God."[12]

The Gospels record examples of Jesus engaged in solitude, although we don't know if it was necessarily accompanied by silence (Matt 4:1–2; 14:13, 23; Mark 1:35; Luke 6:12–13, cf. Matt 26:36–46). Some reasons you may wish to consider introducing short periods of solitude and silence into your schedule include minimizing distractions in prayer, expressing worship to God, expressing trust in God, and regaining spiritual perspective or seeking God's will on an issue.[13]

There are a number of ways that solitude and silence can be practiced. For example:

i. *Stop excessive noise.* When you are alone in the car, or at home, rather than always having the television or radio on, have no background noise. You could use some of this time to pray or reflect.

ii. *Find periods of silence.* Early in the morning before anyone else in your home is awake, or after others have gone to sleep, sit quietly for at least twenty minutes and reflect or pray. Alternatively, you could go for a walk while remaining silent, again using that time to reflect and pray. Furthermore, you could take advantage of the little moments of solitude that come into your day and redeem those.

iii. *Find quiet places.* Look for places where you can be alone with God—both within your home and outside it (parks, libraries, churches).

iv. *Extended periods of solitude.* Every three months you might try withdrawing for three or four hours specifically to read, pray, think through different issues, and reflect on the

---

12. Barton, "Silence," 749.
13. Whitney, *Spiritual Disciplines*, 227–38.

different facets of your life (goals, direction, spiritual life, relationships).

v. *Spiritual retreat.* You might even try going on a spiritual retreat for one or two days in order to really be alone with God, hear from him through his word, and pray.

Confession

Protestants have rightly rejected the Catholic theology and practice of the confessional box, with the priest acting as an intermediary between the person and God because there is only one mediator between God and people—the Lord Jesus Christ (1 Tim 2:5). If we confess our sins to God the Father, then because of the atoning death of God's Son Jesus, God the Father is faithful and just and promises to forgive our sins (1 John 1:9). Christians should regularly confess their sins to God and receive his forgiveness through faith. Nevertheless, the Scriptures do speak of confessing sins to one another (Jas 5:16; cf. Prov 28:13). For the Christian who is listening to and praying for someone who is confessing their sins to them, it may be one of the ways in which they are following Scripture's injunction to bear one another's burdens (Gal 6:2). John Calvin speaks of the benefits of believers confessing their sins to one another such as receiving counsel and consolation, and helping a fellow believer become reconciled with God and others.[14] German theologian Dietrich Bonhoeffer was a strong advocate of corporate Christian confession, arguing that lack of open confession hindered the fellowship required for genuine Christian community.[15] More recently, Dallas Willard has advocated for the practice of Christians confessing their sins to one another:

> Confession is a discipline that functions within fellowship. In it we let trusted others know our deepest weaknesses and failures. This will nourish our faith in God's provision for our needs through his people, our sense of

14. Calvin, *Institutes*, 3.4.12.
15. Bonhoeffer, *Life Together*, 110–22.

being loved, and our humility before our brothers and sisters. Thus we let some friends in Christ know who we really are, not holding back anything important, but, ideally, allowing complete transparency. We lay down the burden of hiding and pretending, which normally takes up such a dreadful amount of human energy. We engage and are engaged by others in the most profound depths of the soul . . . [T]he bearing of the soul to a mature friend in Christ . . . enables such friends to pray for specific problems and do those things that may be most helpful and redemptive to the one confessing.[16]

What can stop us from confessing our sins to one another is our pride and strong desire to protect our personal reputation. We worry what others will think of us in the present and how they might relate to us in the future. But confession of sin to a *trusted* and *appropriate* believer can lead the way for spiritual healing and growth. There is a lot more that could be said about Christian confession that is beyond the scope of this book—particularly as to how the practice has been abused historically by some people. But if you were to helpfully introduce this practice into your Christian life, some things that you might like to think through first include: What place, if any, do you see for Christians confessing their sins to one another? Who is qualified to listen to a Christian's confession of sin? What things would a person confessing their sins to another be wise to consider first? How comfortable would you feel confessing your sins to another Christian?

Serving

It may seem somewhat unusual to consider "service" as a discipline. Yet, when we think of the purpose of the spiritual disciplines in the light of activities which grow a Christian in Christlikeness then we can begin to envisage how acts of service (particularly menial or unseen ones) can grow parts of our character in unique ways—such as developing humility, patience, and love, and confronting pride,

---

16. Willard, *Spirit of the Disciplines*, 187–88.

irritability, and self-centeredness. Dietrich Bonhoeffer famously remarked, "When Christ calls a man, he bids him come and die."[17] While this may conjure up heroic images of pioneer missionaries serving in far-flung places for the sake of the gospel, or Christians serving in dangerous situations, the death that many Christians are called to is more a case of "death-by-degrees," that is, through many small deaths/acts of service. Whitley further challenges,

> We're drawn to the appeal of service when it holds out the promise of bold adventure, but repelled when it means—as it more often does—feeling banished to serve Christ in a dreary corner of a seeming inconsequential place. To have served Jesus by walking with Him during His three-year ministry would have been a glorious adventure; to have served Him three years earlier as His sweeper and saw-sharpener in the carpenter's shop wouldn't have been as appealing.[18]

Jesus's disciples, at the Last Supper, argued over who among them was considered to be the greatest (Luke 22:24). Richard Foster poignantly reflects on the scene:

> Whenever there is trouble over who is the greatest, there is trouble over who is the least. That is the crux of the matter, isn't it? Most of us know we will never be the greatest; just don't let us be the least. Gathered at the Passover feast, the disciples were keenly aware that someone needed to wash the others' feet. The problem was that the only people who washed feet were the least ... So there they sat, feet caked in dirt ... No one wanted to be considered the least. Then Jesus took a towel and a basin and redefined greatness."[19]

---

17. Quoted in Whitney, *Spiritual Disciplines*, 142.

18. Whitney, *Spiritual Disciplines*, 143. Foster similarly writes, "If we forsake all, we even have the chance of glorious martyrdom. But in service we must experience the many little deaths of going beyond ourselves. Service banishes us to the mundane, the ordinary, the trivial." Foster, *Celebration of Discipline*, 158.

19. Foster, *Celebration of Discipline*, 157.

It's because of the hiddenness, drudgery, and lack of recognition that often results from service that serving needs to be considered a discipline. Serving grates against the opposite sins of laziness and pride. These twin sins so impact our mindset that we don't serve God or others as we should. Rather, we do it more occasionally, or when it's convenient, or when there is something in it for ourselves (Mark 10:35-45; Luke 10:38-42; 1 Pet 4:10-11; John 13:1-17).[20]

Serving is not an optional extra for the Christian, and forms part of the good works we were each created to do (Eph 2:10). Not *all* serving is meant to be difficult or drudgery—for that would make the Christian life a fairly joyless one—but some service is. Within the church, serving may be in public activities such as preaching, leading, music, and training, but can equally be through cleaning toys in the nursery, operating the sound or data equipment, or washing the dishes and emptying the bins after morning tea. Outside the church walls serving might include babysitting a child so a young mum can have a break, cooking a meal for someone who is sick, visiting someone who is ill, and living with a servant attitude in your home.[21] The key behind serving as a discipline lies in our attitude. If we do it so as to be seen by others, or out of a sense of duty, then it loses its spiritual value as a discipline. Rather, we need our mindset to reflect that found in Col 3:23-24, "Whatever you do, work at it with all your heart, as working for the Lord, not for human masters, since you know that you will receive an inheritance from the Lord as a reward. It is the Lord Christ you are serving."

Simplicity

The spiritual discipline of simplicity is "an *inward* reality that results in an *outward* lifestyle."[22] While related to poverty, it is far

---

20. Whitney, *Spiritual Disciplines*, 143-44.
21. Whitney, *Spiritual Disciplines*, 143.
22. Foster, *Celebration of Discipline*, 100. Emphasis his.

greater than the renunciation of personal goods attributed to a vow of poverty. The outward display of simplicity must reflect the inward state of the heart that desires more than anything to seek first the kingdom of God and his righteousness. Richard Foster poignantly comments, "The person who does not seek the kingdom first does not seek it at all. Worthy as all other concerns may be, the moment *they* become the focus of our efforts they become idolatry."[23] Seeking first God's kingdom is met regularly with an accompanying freedom from anxiety (Matt 6:25-34).[24] Simplicity involves simplicity of living, speaking, and being. Foster again captures the heart of simplicity when he writes:

> Experiencing the inward reality liberates us outwardly. Speech becomes truthful and honest. The lust for status and position is gone because we no longer need status and position. We cease from showy extravagance not on the grounds of being unable to afford it, but on the grounds of principle. Our goods become available to others ... [We lose our] insane attachment to things.[25]

Simplicity cuts against the grain of our consumerist culture that tells us that we need to have the latest technology, an up-to-the-season wardrobe and so on. The Bible speaks powerfully against such a mindset, demonstrating that a person's attitude to wealth is not just an individual matter but something that comes under God's authority. Everything in this world, including our possessions, are owned by God and are to be used for his glory (Ps 24:1-2). Our attitude towards what we have demonstrates the state of our heart towards God (Matt 6:21). We know that we cannot love both God *and* money but we feel the pull of trying to love both (Matt 6:24). We desire to have far more than we need, resulting in internal and external tensions (Jas 4:1-2). We

---

23. Foster, *Celebration of Discipline*, 107.

24. Foster, *Celebration of Discipline*, 107. Foster identifies three inner attitudes of simplicity: i) receiving what we have as a gift from God; ii) knowing that it is God's business, not ours to care for what we have; iii) to have our goods available to others. Foster, *Celebration of Discipline*, 108-9.

25. Foster, *Celebration of Discipline*, 100.

commend people who live simply, or who sacrifice for the sake of the kingdom, yet deep down think that this sort of lifestyle is for other people rather than for us.

As I was driving to work this morning the radio was ablaze with discussion about the annual online shopping frenzy that is about to take place today with amazing bargains that traditionally mark the beginning of the Christmas shopping season. The radio announcers were asking each other what items they were going to buy, and what might be the most popular purchases across the country in general. But in an unusual moment of clarity, one of the announcers asked, "I wonder how many of the things people will buy today do they actually need?" Our culture is awash with consumerism. It is the air we breathe, and the air our *children* breathe. One of the things I particularly struggle with in regards to this discipline is how to implement this in my home. Like many parents, I don't mind so much missing out myself but don't want my children to. So how do I teach them to live with less and be *content* to live with less, when their peers don't? Jesus said, "Where your treasure is, there your heart will be also" (Matt 6:21). There are many things Jesus said that still elude me—but not this one.

How might we begin to make progress in this area? What might be some possible next steps to make simplicity a genuine part of our lifestyle rather than just an occasional event? The starting point has to be our hearts. Our *attitude* towards possessions dictates our *practice*. To take Foster's phrase, we need to lose our insane attachment to things.[26] We need a renovation of our hearts by God's Spirit—which I suspect for many of us on this issue will be a somewhat painful process. But further to this, in *Celebration of Discipline*, Foster suggests ten guiding principles for living a simplified life, six of which I have included here as somewhere you might like to start:[27]

---

26. Foster, *Celebration of Discipline*, 100.

27. Foster, *Celebration of Discipline*, 110–16. See also Willard, *Divine Conspiracy*, 203–14.

i. Buy things because of how useful they are, rather than for the status they might bring (how much they might impress others). You don't need the biggest or best, but the most functional. For example, only buy the clothes you need, not what you want to keep up with the latest fashion.
ii. Reject anything that you are addicted to: non-nutritional drinks, chocolate, shoes, clothes.
iii. Develop the habit of giving things away. *Deaccumulate*, for example, many of us could get rid of half of our wardrobe and not feel it. Sort through what you have that you are not using and give it away.
iv. Resist the temptation to have the latest gadgets.
v. Learn to enjoy things without owning them. Enjoy public spaces and libraries!
vi. Develop a deeper appreciation for nature. Get out amongst God's creation rather than a cinema.

What is something that you can do to make simplicity a greater part of your life? What things could you give away this week that you don't need?

Chapter 6

Spiritual Gifts

Introduction

SPIRITUAL GIFTS ARE A neglected part of Christian teaching in many churches, yet are an important aspect of Christian discipleship, service, and growth. We each have different gifts, according to the grace of God given to us (Rom 12:6). Lists of gifts are recorded in four passages (Rom 12:3–8; 1 Cor 12–14; Eph 4:11–16; 1 Pet 4:9–11). These lists overlap at points and are illustrative rather than exhaustive. The purpose of the gifts is not self-aggrandizement but rather the building up of the church.[1] While much has been written about spiritual gifts it has rarely been approached from the perspective of spiritual growth. What we contend, however, is that being clear about the issue of spiritual gifts, understanding what your gifts might be, and sacrificially using your gifts in ways that glorify God not only builds up the body of Christ but grows you in Christian maturity and service. In this final chapter we will examine the issue of spiritual gifts from this perspective.

---

1. Schreiner, *Spiritual Gifts*, 16. Schreiner is a cessationist but writes with an irenic spirit when discussing the miraculous gifts and authors with whom he disagrees. In a recent article, Bruce Compton, a fellow cessationist, while agreeing with much of Schreiner's thesis, critiques two aspects of Schreiner's cessationist argument from 1 Cor 13:8–13 before offering his own defence of cessationism. Compton, "First Corinthians 13," 31–49.

The Nature of Spiritual Gifts

As previously mentioned, spiritual gifts are supernatural, God-given abilities distributed by God the Father, God the Son, and God the Holy Spirit to the Christian for the purpose of building up the body of Christ, and for encouraging and unifying the church (Eph 4:12–16; 1 Cor 12:4–6, 25–26; 14:1–40).[2] We are not told how God determines who receives particular gifts but simply that he gives gifts to each person just as he determines (Rom 12:6; 1 Cor 12:11).[3] We need to trust God for his distribution of the gifts. The recipients of these acts of grace should not be disappointed with the gifts God has given them, nor be jealous of other believers who have particular gifts that they do not.[4] A believer's gifts do not make them superior or inferior to others.[5] Rather, believers are all members of "the body of Christ"—a body made up of many parts (1 Cor 12:12, 14). Just as God has so arranged the parts in a human body so that they function exactly how he wants them to, so he has distributed gifts across his church so that it functions exactly how he wants it to (1 Cor 12:18). All gifts are important and necessary for the functioning of the body, but while all members of the body are equal, all gifts are not.[6] Gifts

---

2. Schreiner, *Spiritual Gifts*, 16, 36, 47. This definition is contra Kenneth Berding who argues that spiritual gifts are not Spirit-given *abilities* but rather Spirit-given *ministries* (with "ministries" referring to "any edificatory activity in the Christian community which serves to build up the Christian community"). Berding, "Confusing Word and Concept," 39, 46–50.

3. Garland, *1 Corinthians*, 560; Turner, *Holy Spirit*, 268, 269; Schreiner, *Spiritual Gifts*, 16.

4. Sam Storms writes, "We need to trust his [i.e., God's] wisdom and his goodness and rest confidently that what he has done is for our best interests individually and for the church's best interests corporately." Storms, *Understanding Spiritual Gifts*, 15. He further adds, "To those who may not have gifts that will bring you into the limelight or put a microphone into your hand, those with the gift of service or mercy or encouragement or giving, remember this: people may not see you, but God does." Storms, *Understanding Spiritual Gifts*, 15.

5. Garland, *1 Corinthians*, 560; Schreiner, *Spiritual Gifts*, 38.

6. For example, in 1 Cor 14:1–4 Paul prioritizes prophecy over speaking in tongues because speaking in tongues speaks to people, not to God. People

are to be desired—particularly the greater gifts like prophecy (1 Cor 12:31; 14:1, 5, 39). Speaking in tongues is permitted but it is not nearly as desirable a gift as that of prophecy (1 Cor 14:19). While a believer cannot choose the spiritual gifts God distributes to them, they should seek to excel in gifts that build up the church without becoming fixated on them (1 Cor 14:12).[7] Whatever gift a believer receives from God should be used to serve others and be conducted as a faithful administration of God's grace in its various forms so that God is glorified in all things (1 Pet 4:10).[8]

Types of Spiritual Gifts

More than twenty spiritual gifts are mentioned in the New Testament, with many commentators agreeing that these lists are illustrative rather than exhaustive.[9] That being said, Schreiner notes that from a New Testament perspective these same commentators find it difficult to know what else to add as a spiritual gift.[10] Spiritual gifts are broadly classified as either *miraculous* or *non-miraculous*, with significant debate regarding whether the miraculous gifts continue today or whether they ceased following the apostolic

---

listening to tongues do not understand what is being said (unless interpretation is also provided), where prophecy can be understood directly and leads to the "strengthening, encouraging and comfort" of the church rather than simply edification of the individual. Paul further encourages the Corinthians to "eagerly desire the greater gifts, implying therefore that there are also lesser gifts."

7. Wilson, "Our Spiritual Gifts," 22.

8. Schreiner, *Spiritual Gifts*, 31–32; Garland, *1 Corinthians*, 576.

9. Page, "Assumptions," 48; Turner, "Spiritual Gifts," 193; Schreiner, *Spiritual Gifts*, 17.

10. Schreiner, *Spiritual Gifts*, 17.

age.[11] Spiritual gifts referred to in the New Testament have been variously categorized, including the following:[12]

  i. *People gifts*: apostles, prophets, evangelists, pastor-teachers (Eph 4:11; 1 Cor 12:28–29)

 ii. *Ministry gifts*: prophecy, teaching, leadership, governing, wisdom, knowledge, faith, healing, miraculous powers, distinguishing between spirits, speaking in different tongues, interpretation of tongues (Rom 12:6–8; 1 Cor 12:8–10, 28–30)

iii. *Supporting gifts*: helping others, encouraging, generosity, showing mercy, hospitality, administration (Rom 12:6–8; 1 Cor 12:28; 1 Pet 4:9–11).

Dispute surrounds whether the gifts listed in the passages above are exhaustive or simply illustrative and whether there may in fact be other gifts God may choose to give.[13] Sam Storms is one who argues for the gift lists as simply illustrative. Part of his argument focuses on 1 Cor 12:4–5 where Paul refers to a "variety" of gifts and "varieties" of service. For Storms, this language suggests the gifts mentioned are representative only.[14] He further proposes intercession, deliverance, and interpretation of dreams and visions

---

11. For an overview of the debate see Gruden, *Miraculous Gifts*. The four views are: cessationist (Richard B. Gaffin Jr.), open but cautious (Robert L. Saucy), third wave (C. Samuel Storms), Pentecostal and charismatic (Douglas A. Oss). A brief summary of these four theological views can be found in Stitzinger, "Spiritual Gifts," 145–49.

12. A similar division by some commentators is: *ministry* gifts (Eph 4:11—people specifically enabled to build up and equip other believers); *manifestation* gifts (the list found in 1 Cor 12:7–10); and *motivational* gifts (found in Rom 12:6–10). Another division is simply *speaking* gifts and *serving* gifts. Storms, *Understanding Spiritual Gifts*, 28, 31.

13. Storms, *Understanding Spiritual Gifts*, 34, 37–40.

14. Similarly, Richard Gaffin states, "We should recognise the breadth of the spiritual gifts. When the lists most often discussed (Rom 12; 1 Cor 12; Eph 4) are compared, we see a certain amount of overlap and yet differences among them. This pattern shows that, whether individually or taken together, they are not exhaustive but provide a representative sampling of gifts. To confine our attention to these lists, as so often happens, is unduly limiting." See Gaffin, "Cessationist View," in Gruden, *Miraculous Gifts*, 61.

as potential examples of further gifts, without insisting that they are. His conclusion is that we should at least be open to the possibility of further gifts not directly listed in the New Testament. Exactly what some of these gifts may be is unclear and has generated significant debate amongst scholars on the cessationist-continuationist spectrum. While it is outside the scope of this book to provide a detailed discussion regarding the various interpretations of the nature of each of the gifts, a brief summary of the oft-cited gifts, drawn largely from Tom Schreiner, is in order.

    i. *Apostles*, in a narrow sense, refers to those who were chosen by Jesus who saw the risen Lord.[15] Some have used the word more broadly to refer to pioneer missionaries.[16]

    ii. *Distinguishing between spirits* may refer to the ability to discern between truth and error, accompanied by a thorough knowledge of the Scriptures (e.g., Acts 16:16–18; 1 John 4:1).[17]

    iii. *Faith* doesn't refer to saving faith (common to all believers) but to "extraordinary faith and vision for the future" (e.g., "faith that can move mountains," 1 Cor 13:2).[18]

    iv. *Generosity* refers to people utilizing their wealth and possessions to assist others.[19]

    v. *Healings and miracles* seem to refer to supernatural acts carried on by someone with some regularity.[20]

    vi. *Helping others* refers to the rendering of practical assistance to people.[21]

---

15. Stitzinger, "Spiritual Gifts," 166–67, 170–71.
16. Schreiner, *Spiritual Gifts*, 26–27.
17. Schreiner, *Spiritual Gifts*, 22–23.
18. Schreiner, *Spiritual Gifts*, 21–22; Garland, *1 Corinthians*, 581.
19. Schreiner, *Spiritual Gifts*, 25.
20. Saucy, "Open But Cautious," 129–31; Schreiner, *Spiritual Gifts*, 22.
21. Schreiner, *Spiritual Gifts*, 23.

SPIRITUAL GIFTS

vii. *Leadership* refers to being able to lead and direct others in such a way that they follow.[22]

viii. *Prophecy* refers to declaring God's word. Some equate this to preaching. Others distinguish it from preaching (where God's word is exposited and explained) and see it as communicating spontaneous revelations from God.[23]

ix. *Showing mercy* refers to people who have the sensitivity and insight to minister to those who are hurting or in pain.[24]

x. *Teaching* equates to *"words of wisdom"* and *"words of knowledge"* and accords to the exegeting, explaining, and expounding of God's word (a truth already revealed).[25]

xi. *Tongues* has been described variously as the miraculous ability to speak in another language unknown to the speaker, or the speaking of some heavenly language, or both.[26]

xii. *Wisdom* may refer to special God-given insight into the way God is working out his purposes in the world through Jesus Christ, as well as having special insight to speak into a particular situation.[27]

Spiritual Gifts and the Believer

Every believer has at least one spiritual gift, but God may grant a person multiple gifts according to his sovereign will (1 Cor 12:6–7, 11; Rom 12:6; 1 Pet 4:10–11).[28] Spiritual gifts are given,

---

22. Schreiner equates leadership and administration (Schreiner, *Spiritual Gifts*, 24) but this is unlikely to be the case. Rather, they are distinct gifts. Though a leader may have some administrative ability, administrators more often tend to be better managers than leaders.

23. Schreiner, *Spiritual Gifts*, 96–99; Saucy, "Open But Cautious," 127–28.

24. Schreiner, *Spiritual Gifts*, 24–25.

25. Schreiner, *Spiritual Gifts*, 19–21.

26. Saucy, "Open But Cautious," 131–35.

27. Garland, *1 Corinthians*, 581.

28. Sanou, "Spiritual Gifts," 85; Schreiner, *Spiritual Gifts*, 31, 81–82; Storms,

not earned nor based on merit.[29] Gifts are to be used for the glory of God and for building up the body of Christ rather than for self-aggrandizement (1 Pet 4:10–11; Rom 12:6–8).[30] Spiritual gifts do not come fully developed but mature over time, and so believers need to use their spiritual gifts in order for them to develop. While gifts may be given at conversion, it is possible that God may grant gifts subsequent to conversion as part of equipping the believer for a particular task or role (e.g., 2 Tim 1:6).[31] Gifts are not necessarily permanent. Gifts that are not used can be lost (Matt 25:14–30). Spiritual gifts can also be misused (e.g., tongues in 1 Cor 12, 14) and Christians will be held to account for how they are used (Matt 25:14–30).[32] Christians should maximize the use of their gifts and devote themselves to the work God has given them to do—but exercise their gifts with love (1 Cor 13:1–8).[33]

Natural Talents Versus Spiritual Gifts

Natural talents and spiritual gifts are often understood as distinct from one another. In this view natural talents are considered *physical* abilities which allow you to do certain things (e.g., play music, paint, build, lead etc.) while spiritual gifts are considered *spiritual* abilities which allow you to do certain things.[34] James Stitzinger

---

Understanding Spiritual Gifts, 40–44.

29. Storms, *Understanding Spiritual Gifts*, 42.

30. Garland, *1 Corinthians*, 578; Storms, *Understanding Spiritual Gifts*, 43–44.

31. Storms, *Understanding Spiritual Gifts*, 47.

32. Sanou, "Spiritual Gifts," 85.

33. Turner, *Holy Spirit*, 269; Schreiner, *Spiritual Gifts*, 67–68, 71.

34. William McRae exemplifies this view when he states: "[T]alents may and ought to be dedicated to the Lord to be used for His glory and in His service, but they must always be considered consecrated talents, not spiritual gifts." McRae, *Dynamics*, 20–21, quoted in Stitzinger, "Spiritual Gifts," 157. Stitzinger further adds, "In an accompanying chart McRae notes that spiritual gifts are different from natural talents in that they are independent of hereditary considerations, are probably possessed from conversion, and are given for the purpose of benefiting mankind on the spiritual rather than the natural

SPIRITUAL GIFTS

highlights that while this distinction may hold true when evaluating so-called "miraculous" gifts, difficulties arise when universally applying this distinction to so-called "non-miraculous" gifts such as helps/service or administration. Stitzinger, while maintaining a distinction between natural talents and spiritual gifts, nevertheless sees overlap between the two whereby the Spirit can work through a person's natural talents to such an extent that these talents become spiritual gifts.[35] His framework for understanding the relationship between talents and gifts has three parts: (1) God gives abilities/talents to all people irrespective of their spiritual status; (2) subsequent to Christian conversion the Holy Spirit works through the abilities/talents of the believer so that these are then dedicated for use for God's glory rather than their own; (3) during the period of the early church there were special, supernatural, extraordinary gifts bestowed on the believer (which do not continue today). For him, there is no distinction between dedicated abilities and spiritual gifts.[36]

While drawing on some of Stitzinger's insights, we envisage talents and gifts as something more on a sliding scale, with three categories: (1) talents that God gives each person; (2) talents which a person, having become a believer, dedicate to God and so are utilized by the Spirit for the glory of God; (3) additional spiritual gifts which God specifically gives to the believer at or subsequent to conversion.

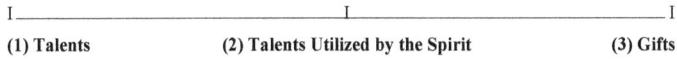

(1) Talents   (2) Talents Utilized by the Spirit   (3) Gifts

---

level." Stitzinger, "Spiritual Gifts," 157.
35. Stitzinger, "Spiritual Gifts," 158.
36. Stitzinger, "Spiritual Gifts," 158.

Identifying Spiritual Gifts

Identifying natural talents or abilities is something we do instinctively over time. As we grow we (or those around us) begin to see what we are good at, what we excel in, what seems to come more naturally, and what we enjoy doing, and from this discern our natural talents. Personal dedication, resources, and opportunity for developing these all contribute to whether our natural talents are enhanced or not. The question is then raised regarding the process for discovering our spiritual gifts—whether we simply follow the same process as for natural talents or take a different approach (such as using spiritual gift inventories). A further question is whether it even matters whether or not we know what our gifts are. Does God just want us to serve him as need and opportunity arise, without us having complete knowledge of the gifts he has given?

At one level, the growing Christian is one who desires to serve and follow in the footsteps of their master (Mark 10:45; John 13:4–5, 14–15; Phil 2:5–8). As already stated, we tend to be drawn to great tasks rather than menial ones, and at least some of our lack of serving may not be so much an issue of *gifting* as *attitude*. Sometimes we just have to be willing to serve in the children's ministry at our church, or be on the cleaning roster, or give extra financially, because there is a need and we do have the time or means to do it, even though it might not fall into the category of one of our spiritual gifts. Interestingly, it can be while we are serving that we actually discover spiritual gifts we didn't realise we had.

Yet, at another level, serving in line with our spiritual giftings can bring an increased measure of joy, blessing, and growth for the body of Christ as well as for ourselves. There is great value in knowing and using our spiritual gifts, and a good starting point for doing this is by making an honest evaluation of *ourselves*. Schreiner helpfully elaborates:

> The need to discern our calling is immensely practical and applies to so many areas of life. You may not be gifted musically, or an eloquent speaker, but you notice those in pain and reach out to them (mercy!), or willingly serve

SPIRITUAL GIFTS

behind the scenes (helps!). We are to bloom where God has planted us and find the niche where God has placed us, and then live with all our strength for God's glory . . . A realistic assessment of our lives and talents and gifts brings great contentment about our place in life if we rest in God . . . We are to think in a sensible way about ourselves and should not think too highly about ourselves . . . We should not long, then, for greatness God doesn't intend us to have, but should find contentment in our lives by not overestimating our gifts or wishing for gifts that have not been given to us.[37]

An honest evaluation of our gifts by *others* can also yield great dividends. Again, Schreiner writes:

The Lord calls us to assess our gifts realistically, and here is where other people can help us, for our gifts don't just reflect what we think about ourselves. Other members of the body of Christ can and must help us discern and confirm gifts in our lives. Sometimes they help us see that the gift we thought we had isn't the area [in which] we should concentrate our energies after all.[38]

Furthermore, spiritual gift inventories have some potential at a general level to support the methods mentioned above—depending on the one you use. These inventories are self-assessment tools designed to help Christians identify their spiritual gifts, usually through answering a series of questions where the participant is asked to score themselves on various characteristics.[39] Following the spiritual gift self-assessment first developed by Peter Wagner in *Your Spiritual Gifts Can Help Your Church Grow*, many such self-assessments have been developed since, and attracted widespread use.[40]

H. T. Page, following Kenneth Berding, argues against the use of spiritual gift inventories. His reasons include that they are

---

37. Schreiner, *Spiritual Gifts*, 35, 36.
38. Schreiner, *Spiritual Gifts*, 35.
39. Page, "Assumptions," 39.
40. Wagner, *Your Spiritual Gifts*.

based on wrong assumptions regarding the nature of spiritual gifts, unduly restrict themselves to the gift lists found in the New Testament,[41] and contain a lack of clarity regarding what was meant by the different terms recorded in these lists (e.g., administration, prophecy, wisdom etc.)[42]

Gaffin seeks to reframe the approach to identifying personal spiritual gifts when he writes:

> One way *not* to proceed [with discovering your spiritual gifts] is to take the "spiritual inventory" approach and ask: What is it that I would like for my spiritual speciality? What is "my thing" spiritually that sets me apart from other believers? The New Testament would have us take a more functional or situational approach to identifying spiritual gifts. The key question to ask is this: What needs are there within the situation where God has placed me? What in the circumstances where I find myself are the particular opportunities for serving others. In light of the dual profile of 1 Pet 4:11, what are the specific ways in which I can minister the gospel of Jesus Christ in word or deed.[43]

He proceeds to suggest that approaching the issue that way, alongside careful personal reflection, prayer, and input from fellow

---

41. Page writes, "There are obvious difficulties with any tool that excludes areas of ministry that God may be calling individuals to fill. Persons using the instrument may be tempted to limit their consideration to the gifts that the inventory is designed to test for and consequently ignore opportunities to which they could and should respond." Page, "Assumptions," 49. Cooper and Blakeman, "Spiritual Gifts," 39–44 also challenge the seemingly scientific nature of spiritual gift inventories in general through an evaluation of the Motivational Spiritual Gifts Inventory (MGI) in particular. They conclude that any questionnaire that has not undergone rigorous psychometric development has significant limitations.

42. Page, "Assumptions," 39, 48–49. He further challenges the assumptions behind the idea that clear distinctions can be made between related terms and an assumption concerning which of the gifts are continuous today. While keeping that in mind, from reviewing various inventories, one that may be worth considering is: https://gifts.churchgrowth.org/spiritual-gifts-survey/gifts-survey/.

43. Gaffin, "Cessationist View," in Gruden, *Miraculous Gifts*, 62.

believers (particularly church leaders) will be a significant help for the Christian seeking to identify and use their spiritual gifts.[44]

Along similar lines, Sydney Page suggests the following approach for discovering your spiritual gifts:[45]

i. Recognize that every member of the body of Christ has an important contribution to make to extend God's kingdom.

ii. Look around and see what needs exist within the community you are serving in and evaluate which ones you might be capable of fulfilling.

iii. Pay close attention to what others in the community might see as your gifts, or where they could see you serving. As we are engaging in Christian service, others may see a gift in us long before we ourselves are aware of it. Occasionally, others recognize that we don't possess a gift we think we have.

iv. Get busy serving, as Christians often discover their gifts in this context.

To these I would add:

v. Pay attention to what you enjoy doing and what areas of ministry in your life God seems to be using for his glory.

vi. Be open to using a spiritual gift inventory in combination with the steps suggested above.

Spiritual Gifts and Spiritual Growth

God provides spiritual gifts so that believers can strengthen and encourage one another, and for the purpose of God incrementally transforming them into the image of Christ. The church grows into what God has designed though the godly use of the gifts he has provided.[46] God's goal for the church is to achieve unity of the

---

44. Gaffin, "Cessationist View," 62–63.
45. Page, "Assumptions," 59.
46. Storms, *Understanding Spiritual Gifts*, xvi.

faith and of the knowledge of the Son of God (Eph 4:7–16). This isn't something that happens automatically but rather occurs as each believer contributes to the spiritual growth of their fellow believers.[47] Using our spiritual gifts not only contribute to our own spiritual growth, but to the spiritual growth of other believers. The essential role of fellow believers in the context of utilization of our spiritual gifts needs to be stressed. As highlighted earlier, our spiritual growth doesn't happen in isolation. Rather, as members of the body of Christ, as each member grows, so does the body. The growth of the body occurs both as we love and serve each other, as well as through use of the gifts God has given us. Gifts and growth go together, with the gifts an essential way in which the power of the Holy Spirit works among us to grow the body. We each have our part to play in this, and we grow as we play our part. The gifts and fruit of the Spirit are therefore complementary: the fruit is Christlikeness, but this does not exist in isolation. Rather, the fruit of love, joy, peace, patience, kindness, goodness, faithfulness, gentleness, and self-control are displayed and developed in the context of serving one another. The gifts are part of this service and as we serve we grow in Christlikeness.

That being said, having a particular gift does not mean Christians can demand the right to use it in a particular context. God is not a God of disorder but of order and peace (1 Cor 14:33). In a local church context, for example, there may be multiple people with a particular gift and limited opportunities for that gift to be exercised there. Sometimes the most loving thing for someone to do in that context is not push their way forward so that they get to exercise their gifts (e.g., preaching, teaching) but cheerfully allow others to serve in that way instead. Such a person may then pray and seek other opportunities to exercise their gifts. If we are going to grow, we must come to know and use the spiritual gifts God has given us. They are an important part of our obedience to God's command, "through love serve one another" (Gal 5:13). Love must be our governing motivation, and our ultimate goal, the building

---

47. Storms, *Understanding Spiritual Gifts*, xvi.

up of the church to the glory of God.[48] Gifts exercised in a way that leads to self-promotion, and where love of self exceeds love of God and love of neighbor undermines such a person's spirituality. Love is the hallmark of the spiritually mature Christian.[49]

---

48. Thistleton, *First Epistle*, 1035; Gardner amplifies: "[Spiritual gifts] only make sense when used in a context where people are marked out as the Lord's by 'love.'" Gardner, *1 Corinthians*, 557.

49. Gardner, *1 Corinthians*, 562.

Conclusion

WHILE I WAS AT university there was a particular place I loved to go when I needed time to reflect and pray. It was a section of a park where there was an old tree. I don't know how old the tree was—possibly some hundreds of years. I don't even know what sort of tree it was. It stood roughly forty-foot high, with branches that spread out like a canopy to provide lots of shade as I sat underneath. But what I most loved about that tree was the thick trunk. It was broad, gnarled, with roots spreading out to the waiting earth below. Just running my hand over the trunk made me feel connected to something greater than myself. Something strong. Something solid. Something that had stood the test of time. Over the past thirty years I have visited that spot multiple times when back visiting that city. And while buildings flanking the park have been upgraded or replaced, and even changes made to the park itself, that tree is still there. Solid. Firm. Growing.

The opening Psalm introduces two types of people, the righteous and the wicked, with the character and fate of each regularly described throughout the rest of the Psalter. Psalm 1 begins, "Blessed is the one who does not walk in step with the wicked or stand in the way that sinners take or sit in the company of mockers, but whose delight is in the law of the Lord, and who meditates on his law day and night" (Ps 1:1–2). The person who is truly blessed by God, the righteous, is one who does not allow themselves to be influenced by the values and behavior of those who reject God (Ps 1:5). Rather, they allow themselves to be shaped by

CONCLUSION

God as they regularly meditate on God's word. In doing so they are changed—transformed into something remarkable and useful: "That person is like a tree planted by streams of water, which yields its fruit in season and whose leaf does not wither—whatever they do prospers" (Ps 1:3). This tree continues being nourished as its roots draw on the life-giving water of the surrounding streams. It continues growing and bearing fruit, year in, year out. Its trunk doesn't dry up. Its leaves don't wither. No matter what storms it faces, like the house built on the rock it will not fall over for it is built on a solid foundation (Matt 7:24–25).

This book has sought to explore some of the contours of the Christian's spiritual journey. We have seen that this journey of spiritual formation is a Spirit-led and believer-response process whereby individuals and communities grow into ever-greater Christlikeness in the community of and for the sake of the church and the world. We've also considered some of the means God uses to bring about this spiritual transformation: the Holy Spirit, people, circumstances, suffering, various spiritual practices known as the spiritual disciplines, and spiritual gifts. I don't know where you are at in your spiritual journey—whether just starting out, getting close to the finish line, or somewhere in-between. But whatever stage you are at, the good news is that God is continuing to be at work in your life. He is not like those builders you sometimes hear about in the news or current affairs shows who build half a house and then abscond with people's money. God always finishes what he starts (Phil 1:6). And one day that journey of transformation will be complete as we see him face-to-face, and marvel anew at his mercy and grace which has transformed us into his image.

Bibliography

Barton, Ruth Hayley. "Silence." In *Dictionary of Christian Spirituality*, edited by Glen C. Scorgie, 749–50. Grand Rapids: Zondervan, 2011.
———. "Solitude." In *Dictionary of Christian Spirituality*, edited by Glen C. Scorgie, 762–63. Grand Rapids: Zondervan, 2011.
Bennett, Arthur, ed. *The Valley of Vision: A Collection of Puritan Prayers and Devotions*. Edinburgh: The Banner of Truth Trust, 1975.
Berding, Kenneth. "Confusing Word and Concept in 'Spiritual Gifts': Have We Forgotten James Barr's Exhortations?" *Journal of the Evangelical Theological Society* 43, no. 1 (2000) 37–51.
Boa, Kenneth. *Conformed to His Image: Biblical and Practical Approaches to Spiritual Formation*. Grand Rapids: Zondervan, 2001.
Bonhoeffer, Dietrich. *Life Together: The Classic Exploration of Christian Community*. New York: HarperCollins, 1954.
Calvin, John. *Commentaries on the Epistles of Paul to the Galatians and Ephesians*. Translated by William Pringle. Edinburgh: Calvin Translation Society, 1855.
———. *Institutes of the Christian Religion*. Vol 1. Translated by Ford Lewis Battles. Philadelphia: Westminster, 1960.
Carson, D. A. *Praying With Paul: A Call to Spiritual Reformation*. 2nd ed. Grand Rapids, MI: Baker, 2014.
Chester, Tim. *You Can Pray*. Nottingham: IVP, 2014.
Chin, Richard. *How to Read the Bible Better*. Sydney: Matthias Media, 2021.
Compton, R. Bruce. "First Corinthians 13 and the Cessation of Miraculous Gifts: A Critique of Thomas Schreiner's Spiritual Gifts: What They Are and Why They Matter." *Detroit Baptist Seminary Journal* 25 (2020) 31–49.
Cooper, Stewart E., and Stephen D. Blakeman. "Spiritual Gifts: A Psychometric Extension." *Journal of Psychology and Theology* 22, no. 1 (1994) 39–44.
Demarest, Bruce. *Satisfy Your Soul: Restoring the Heart of Christian Spirituality*. Colorado Springs: NavPress, 1999.

BIBLIOGRAPHY

DeVries, Brian A. "Spiritual Gifts for Biblical Church Development: The Holy Spirit Working through Believers to Build Up the Body of Christ." *Puritan Reformed Journal* 13, no. 2 (2021) 181–203.

Dickson, John. *If I Were God I'd End All the Pain: Struggling with Evil, Suffering and Faith*. Kingsford: Matthias Media, 2001.

Foster, Richard J. *Celebration of Discipline: The Path to Spiritual Growth*. London: Hodder and Stoughton, 2008.

———. *Streams of Living Water*. San Francisco: HarperCollins, 1998.

Gaffin, Richard B., Jr., et al. *Are Miraculous Gifts for Today? Four Views*. Grand Rapids: Zondervan, 1996.

Gardner, Paul D. *1 Corinthians*. Zondervan Exegetical Commentary on the New Testament. Grand Rapids: Zondervan, 2018.

Garland, David E. *1 Corinthians*. Baker Exegetical Commentary on the New Testament 7. Grand Rapids: Baker, 2003.

Green, Gene L. *Jude and 2 Peter*. Baker Exegetical Commentary on the New Testament 22. Grand Rapids: Baker, 2008.

Greenman, Jeffrey P. "Spiritual Formation in Theological Perspective: Classic Issues, Contemporary Challenges." In *Life in the Spirit: Spiritual Formation in Theological Perspective*, edited by Jeffrey P. Greenman and George Kalantzis, 23–35. Downers Grove: IVP Academic, 2010.

Howard, Evan B. *A Guide to Christian Spiritual Formation: How Scripture, Spirit, Community, and Mission Shape Our Souls*. Grand Rapids: Baker Academic, 2018.

Keller, Timothy. *Walking with God through Pain and Suffering*. London: Hodder and Stoughton, 2015.

Kelly, J. N. D. *Golden Mouth: The Story of John Chrysostom: Ascetic, Preacher, Bishop*. Grand Rapids: Baker, 1995.

Linder, Robert D. "Fast, Fasting." In *Evangelical Dictionary of Theology*, edited by Walter A. Elwell, 437–39. 2nd ed. Grand Rapids: Baker, 2001.

Lovelace, Richard F. "Evangelical Spirituality: A Church Historians Perspective." *Journal of the Evangelical Theological Society* 31, no. 1 (1988) 25–35.

MacDonald, George. "Man's Difficulty Concerning Prayer." In *Creation in Christ*, edited by Rolland Hein. Wheaton: Harold Shaw, 1976.

Matthews, S. H. *Christian Fasting: Biblical and Evangelical Perspectives*. Langham: Lexington, 2015.

Mayer, Wendy, and Pauline Allen. *John Chrysostom*. London: Routledge, 2000.

McRay, Barrett W., et al. "Spiritual Formation and Soul Care in the Department of Christian Formation and Ministry at Wheaton College." *Journal of Spiritual Formation and Soul Care* 11, no. 2 (2018) 271–95.

Miles, Margaret M. "Towards a New Asceticism." *The Christian Century* (October 28, 1981) 1097–98.

Motyer, Alec. *Isaiah*. Leicester: IVP, 1999.

Mulholland, M. Robert, Jr. *Invitation to a Journey: A Road Map for Spiritual Formation*. Rev. ed. Downers Grove: IVP, 2016.

BIBLIOGRAPHY

Page, Sydney H. T. "The Assumptions Behind Spiritual Gifts Inventories." *Didaskalia* 22 (September 2002) 39–59.

Prince, Andrew James. *Contextualization of the Gospel: Towards an Evangelical Approach in the Light of Scripture and the Church Fathers*. Eugene: Wipf & Stock, 2017.

Sanou, Boubakar. "Spiritual Gifts, Pastoring, and Gender: An Ongoing Dialogue." *Journal of Applied Christian Leadership* 11, no. 2 (2019) 84–91.

Schaeffer, Francis A. *True Spirituality*. Wheaton: Tyndale House, 1971.

Schreiner, Thomas R. *Spiritual Gifts: What They Are and Why They Matter*. Nashville: B&H, 2018.

Stitzinger, James F. "Spiritual Gifts: Definitions and Kinds." *The Masters Seminary Journal* 14, no. 2 (Fall 2003) 143–76.

Storms, Sam. *Understanding Spiritual Gifts: A Comprehensive Guide*. Grand Rapids: Zondervan, 2020.

Straw, Gordon J. "Native Thought, Suffering, and Spiritual Formation as Theological Education." *Currents in Theology and Mission* 47, no. 1 (January 2020) 10–16.

Thistleton, Anthony C. *The First Epistle to the Corinthians*. New International Greek Testament Commentary. Grand Rapids: Eerdmans, 2000.

Thompson, Marjorie. *Soul Feast: An Invitation to the Christian Spiritual Life*. Rev. ed. Louisville: Westminster John Knox, 2014. https://brisbaneschooloftheology.eplatform.co/title/9781611645378/epub.

Turner, Max. *The Holy Spirit and Spiritual Gifts: Then and Now*. Carlisle: Paternoster, 1996.

———. "Spiritual Gifts and Spiritual Formation in 1 Corinthians and Ephesians." *Journal of Pentecostal Theology* 22 (2013) 187–205.

Wagner, C. Peter. *Your Spiritual Gifts Can Help Your Church Grow*. Ventura: Regal, 1979.

Whitney, Donald S. *Spiritual Disciplines for the Christian Life*. Rev. ed. Carol Stream: NavPress, 2014.

Willard, Dallas. *Renovation of the Heart: Putting on the Character of Christ*. 20th Anniversary ed. Colorado Springs: NavPress, 2021.

———. *The Spirit of the Disciplines: Understanding How God Changes Lives*. New York: HarperCollins, 1988. https://ebookcentral.proquest.com/lib/bst/reader.action?docID=6821409.

Wilson, Andrew. "Our Spiritual Gifts Have an Expiration Date." *Christianity Today* 61, no. 5 (June 2017) 22.

www.ingramcontent.com/pod-product-compliance
Lightning Source LLC
Chambersburg PA
CBHW070101100426
42743CB00012B/2618